CONTRA SCANDAL UPDATE

IN CONTEMPT OF CONGRESS

THE REAGAN RECORD ON CENTRAL AMERICA

A CITIZENS' GUIDE

EDITED BY **JOY HACKEL** AND **DANIEL SIEGEL**

WITH PREFACES BY
SENATOR TOM HARKIN AND **GEORGE McGOVERN**

ACKNOWLEDGEMENTS

The editors extend their thanks to the many people who contributed to the original and updated versions of this book. First, we owe our gratitude to the Institute for Policy Studies, particularly to Robert L. Borosage, Philip Brenner and Saul Landau whose continuing support and editorial guidance made this project possible.

We want to thank our contributing editors and researchers: Mary Ellen Fleck, Jeffrey Jackson, Thomas Klubock, Peter Kornbluh, Ellen Nagle, Diana Propper, Rene Riley, and Katie Roberts.

Finally, we thank the following people for their assistance: Raymond Bonner, John Cavanagh, Ruth Chojnacki, the Christic Institute, Betsy Cohn, Colin Danby, Heather Foote, Jim Hershberg, John Kelly, William LeoGrande, Allan Nairn, Jeff Nason, the National Security Archive, NISGUA, Reggie Norton, Jay Peterzell, Rick Reinhard, Donna Rich and George Rogers.

1st Printing: April, 1985
2nd Printing: October, 1985
2nd Edition 1st Printing: October, 1987

Copies of this book are available from the Institute for Policy Studies, 1901 Q St., NW, Washington, DC 20009.

Design: Jeffrey Jackson
Maps: John Yanson

TABLE · OF · CONTENTS

Introduction
67

NICARAGUA
74

EL SALVADOR
93

HONDURAS
107

GUATEMALA
117

Appendix: Possible Violations of Law
128

Part 1:
A Citizens' Guide to the Contra Scandal

PREFACE

TO THE SECOND EDITION

In his State of the Union address earlier this year, President Reagan heralded the 200th anniversary of the our constitution. He praised the work of our founding fathers and noted that he had read not only our constitution but the constitution of other countries.

The President may indeed have read our constitution, but, as revelations of the Iran/contra arms sale reveal, he does not understand it.

On foreign policy, the constitution created an "invitation to struggle" between the President and Congress, not an invitation to deceive.

The Iran/contra affair has undermined all conventional notions of executive authority and the foreign policy process. The Reagan administration--including the President himself--did far more than "wink and nod" at the so-called private efforts to assist the contras. The White House became the nerve center for shady operations that coordinated the work of a network of ex-generals, old CIA hands and soldiers of fortune to keep the contra war going at a time when such activity was outlawed by Congress.

President Reagan's responsibility in this affair transcends lying and law-breaking. By ignoring the fragile but vital separation of powers between Congress and the executive, the President demeans the very nature of our form of government.

The secret contra resupply operation, organized by the White House to circumvent congressional and public opposition to the President's "dirty little war" in Central America, bypassed and denied Congress its two greatest constitutional powers--the sole authority to appropriate funds and the power to declare war.

Perhaps we should not be surprised. The use of ex-generals and sultans to spearhead a foreign policy apparatus is a logical extension of the Reagan Doctrine. This policy of Soviet rollback through worldwide sponsorship of counterrevolution has been advanced in Angola, Cambodia and Nicaragua. Its principal instrument is the

CIA and covert operations.

In its zealous (almost religious) pursuit of this doctrine, the Reagan administration has written assassination manuals, mined ports, and created an armed band better at killing innocent peasants than government soldiers. Ronald Reagan has waged his own "holy war" against the alleged Soviet menace, in the process adopting the methods of our enemies. Whoever "wins", if that is possible, America stands to lose its most precious possession, our rule of law.

Americans should have learned a decade ago, with the revelations of Watergate and the Church Committee, that covert operations and the American constitutional system are incompatible. In Nicaragua today, as in Chile and Vietnam a generation ago, those involved in U.S. policy operate in secret, behind a bodyguard of lies, and in violation of international as well as domestic law.

I can think of no better way for Americans to celebrate the Bicentennial than to restore constitutionalism and the rule of law to foreign policy.

Senator Tom Harkin

INTRODUCTION

"There is great deceit or deception practiced in the conduct of [a] covert operation. They are at essence a lie."
Lt. Col. Oliver North
before the Joint Select Committee to Investigate
the Iran/Contra Affair

"Our objective here all along was to withhold information [from Congress]. There's no question about that."
John Poindexter,
before the Joint Select Committee

"I think in hindsight the people that we were deceiving may have been the American public..."
Robert Owen,
Oliver North's liaison with the contras,
before the Joint Select Committee

"The whole art of government consists in the art of being honest."
Thomas Jefferson

In October of 1984, the Institute for Policy Studies began documenting the many deceptions and illegalities that undergirded the Reagan administration's policies in Central America. Even then, the pattern of deceit was clear.

When *In Contempt of Congress* was released at a press conference in April of 1985 by Senators Tom Harkin (D-IA), John Kerry (D-MA) and Rep. Norman Mineta (D-CA), a reporter asked: "If this report is true, shouldn't we be talking about the impeachment of the president?" Senator Harkin slowly approached the podium and replied: "I think you have your finger on it."

The White House responded angrily to Harkin's remark. A representative from Vice President Bush's office was promptly sent over to IPS to buy a copy of our report.

In Contempt of Congress, however, did not provoke widespread high-level reaction. Calls for Congressional hearings went unheeded. Administration officials continued to testify that they were upholding the spirit and letter of the law in Central America, while President Reagan escalated his war against Nicaragua.

Then the Iran/contra scandal exploded. Little did we know just how contemptuous were the activities of the Reagan regime. Only six days before our press conference, Lt. Col. Oliver North wrote a memo to National Security Advisor Robert McFarlane detailing how over $17 million had been secretly raised and spent on the contras since July 1984 when official U.S. government aid to the rebels was banned.

Two weeks after the press conference, Vice President Bush met with Oliver North and Felix Rodriguez (alias Max Gomez), who was the field director of the secret contra resupply network located at the Ilopango air base in El Salvador. Rodriguez began working with the contras in early 1985 after meeting with the Vice President and his staff. Despite irrefutable evidence to the contrary, Bush denies ever having talked with Rodriguez about the contra aid network.

White House lying has been accompanied by a massive propaganda effort to win hearts and minds at home. A month before the press conference, a pro-contra editorial by a Rice University professor appeared in the Wall Street Journal without notice that the writer was secretly paid by the Reagan Administration for his efforts. The next day, a "confidential, eyes-only" memo by the Office of Public Diplomacy for Latin America and the Caribbean described the article as a small example of the State Department's "White Propaganda" operation to sway Congress, the press and the public in support of the contras. This covert propaganda campaign violated a Congressional ban on the use of tax-payer money for unauthorized publicity or propaganda purposes.

The following "Citizens' Guide to the Contra Scandal" deepens the "disturbingly systematic record of White House deceit" documented in our original report. The flood of evidence pouring forth from the Tower Commission, the Joint Select Committee of Congress, other standing congressional committees, investigative reporters and public interest groups underscores just how endemic Reagan administration deception on Central America has been. From the President down to lowly field operatives, stretching across the CIA-Pentagon-State Department-White House axis, the Contragate scandal encompasses a complex and endless web of lying and law-breaking.

This update by no means completes the picture. Focusing solely on U.S. policy toward Central America, and Nicaragua in particular, we have left unexamined the whole Iranian operation, save for the diversion of Iran arms sale profits to the contras. Other questions can be posed about our policy toward Nicaragua. We are not updating Reagan administration untruths concerning El Salvador, Guatemala and Honduras. Over the coming months and years, thousands of other secret documents and memos will undoubtedly surface to darken this already grotesque portrait.

The policy questions remain: What is to be done?

First, as long as the United States backs unpopular regimes and movements in Central America that do not have the support of the U.S. public, this and future administrations will continually bend the truth to defend and promote their policy goals. Backing the brutal and corrupt contra army inherently breeds scandal. Congress must embrace the demands for peace throughout the Americas by ending the failed contra war and learning to live with Nicaragua.

Above all, Contragate demonstrates how waging secret "low-intensity" operations abroad creates high-intensity lawlessness at home. Toppling foreign governments in the name of democracy, as in Nicaragua, invariably undermines our own democracy.

This scandal is a logical extension of the shadow government erected 40 years ago following the Second World War. Based on secrecy, cloak-and-dagger operations, and excessive Executive power, this national security state within our government has become incompatible with openness and accountability--namely democracy. The Iran/contra affair gives Congress the opportunity to begin re-democratizing U.S. foreign policy by debating the very need and purpose of the CIA and the NSC.

Congress, however, must accept its share of the blame for backing covert warfare around the globe. Following the Vietnam-Watergate-CIA scandal period of the mid-1970's, some members of Congress sought to check the national security state by outlawing covert operations. When that effort failed, members settled for establishing Senate and House committees that would monitor covert actions. In practice, "oversight" became a *double entendre* , a rubber stamp for the CIA's clandestine operations. By attempting to ensure that covert operators followed the rules for inherently dubious activity, Congress found itself caught between attempting to simultaneously limit and authorize criminal activity -- to make laws, while allowing the CIA to selectively break them.

Congress can ask the obvious question as it seeks to "restore the system". What system does it want to restore: the forms of government defined in the Constitution, or the national security state? To govern an empire requires an imperial mandate. National security doctrine is designed for imperial practices within the form of an accountable republic. And that mismarriage of government forms has led to "scandals".

To restore the republic and its credibility, Congress and the public must reverse not just the means, but the ends of an imperial foreign policy. There is no consensus in this land for overseas adventures. That sentiment has been reflected in a Congress divided over contra aid. Domestic tranquility requires a lawful and prudent policy, one that accepts not only the limits imposed by substantial opposition at home, but also the right of other people to choose their own forms of government, particularly those living in our "own backyard". President Reagan assumes that the United States can and should control other parts of the world. What Contragate has shown are the limits of U.S. power. When all is said and done, billions of dollars were spent on fighting "dirty little wars" abroad. The real price was untold death and chaos in other lands and the corruption of our own democracy at home.

Daniel Siegel
Joy Hackel

October, 1987

I. THE SECRET CONTRA RESUPPLY NETWORK

ISSUE: Between October, 1984 and October, 1985, the United States Congress enacted the Boland Amendment, which banned the Reagan Administration from providing direct or indirect support for military or paramilitary activities against the government of Nicaragua. Did Reagan Administration officials deceive Congress and violate the law by creating a private military resupply network for the Nicaraguan contras?

ADMINISTRATION POSITION	COUNTEREVIDENCE
"...the actions of the NSC staff were in compliance with both the spirit and the letter of the law regarding support of the Nicaraguan resistance." *John Poindexter,* *National Security Advisor,* *Letter to Rep. Lee Hamilton,* *Chairman, House Select* *Committee on Intelligence,* *July 21, 1986*	"My objective all along was to withhold from the Congress exactly what the [National Security Council] staff was doing in carrying out the President's policy [toward Nicaragua]. ...There was obviously knowledge by the NSC as to what the private organization [supplying the contras] was doing. There was coordination." *John Poindexter,* *Testimony before the Joint Select* *Committee,* *July 17, 1987*
"There is no official or unofficial relationship with any member of the NSC staff regarding fundraising for the Nicaraguan democratic opposition." *Robert McFarlane,* *National Security Advisor,* *Letter to Rep. Lee Hamilton,* *October 7, 1985*	"It appears, however, that Lt Col North did keep the National Security Advisor informed [about the contra resupply operation], first Mr. McFarlane and then VADM [Vice Admiral] Poindexter. On May 15, 1986, VADM Poindexter cautioned North: 'From now on, I don't want you to talk to anybody else, including Casey, except me about any of your operational roles.'" *The Tower Commission Report,* *February, 1987*

"The allegation that Lieutenant Colonel North offered the resistance tactical advice and direction is...patently false...North did not use his influence to facilitate the movement of supplies to the resistance." *Robert McFarlane,* *Letter to Rep. Lee Hamilton,* *October 7, 1985*	"Next week, a sum of $20M [million] will be deposited in the usual acount...it should allow us to bridge the gap between now and when the vote is taken and the funds are turned on again [by Congress]...we can start a regular logistics program of one flight every 10 - 15 days and the steady movement of supplies and ammunition [to the contras]...destroy this letter after reading...We need to make sure that this new financing does <u>not</u> become known. The Congress must believe that there continues to be an urgent need for funding." *Lt. Col. Oliver North,* *Director of Political-Military Affairs,* *National Security Council,* *in undated letter to Robert Owen,* *State Department contract employee*
"Indeed, our actions have been and must be in conformity...with <u>all</u> laws... none of us has solicited funds, facilitated contacts for prospective donors, or otherwise organized or coordinated the military or paramilitary efforts of the resistance." *Robert McFarlane,* *Letter to Rep. Michael Barnes Chairman, House Subcommittee on Western Hemisphere Affairs,* *September 12, 1985*	
	"It is apparent that the 7M [million dollars] remaining will be insufficient to allow the resistance to advance beyond these limited objectives...Efforts should, therefore, be made to seek additional funds from the current donors ($15-20M) which will allow the [contra] force to grow to 30-35,000." *Oliver North,* *Memorandum for Robert McFarlane,* *April 11, 1985*
"I want to assure you that my actions and those of my staff, have been in compliance with both the spirit and the letter of the law. ...There have not been, nor will there be, any expendi-	

tures of NSC funds which would have the effect of supporting directly or indirectly military or paramilitary operations in Nicaragua by any nation, group, organization, movement or individual..."

Robert McFarlane,
Letter to Rep. Michael Barnes,
September 12, 1985

"The very day that Mr. McFarlane wrote me a letter saying in no uncertain terms that there was no truth to these allegations, on that very day, Ollie North was typing memos to Mr. McFarlane and others about his current activities on behalf of the contras. I mean, that's--that's pretty extraordinary."

Rep. Michael Barnes,
on ABC newshow "Nightline",
March 12, 1987

"I can state with deep personal conviction that at no time did I or any other member of the NSC staff violate the letter or spirit of the law."

Robert McFarlane,
Letter to Rep. Lee Hamilton,
September 5, 1985

"On April 11, 1985, LtCol North sent a memorandum to Mr. McFarlane describing two sealifts and two airlifts '[a]s of April 9, 1985'. The memorandum set out the kind of munitions purchased, the quantity, and in some instances the costs. LtCol North also noted that from July, 1984 to April 19, 1985: $17,145,594 has been expended for arms, munitions, combat operations,and support activities.'"

The Tower Commission Report,
February, 1987

McFarlane

ADMINISTRATION POSITION	COUNTEREVIDENCE
"On October 21, 1985 Mr. McFarlane received an inquiry from Congressman Richard Durbin. Congressman Durbin asked: 'Are there any efforts currently underway in the Administration to facilitate the sending of private donations to the contras? McFarlane replied: 'No.'"	"Asked by the Board about the source of such funds, Mr. McFarlane provided a written response that indicated that 'without solicitation' a foreign official offered $1 million a month from what he described as 'personal funds.' At Mr. McFarlane's request, LtCol North provided the numbers of a Contra bank account in Miami. Mr. McFarlane wrote that in 1985, the foreign official [a Saudi] doubled his contribution to $2 million a month, a fact confirmed by two other U.S. officials."
The Tower Commission Report February, 1987	*The Tower Commission Report February 1987*
"NORTH has denied media allegations that SECORD works for him and reiterated this point during the interview. NORTH stated that neither he nor his staff are responsible for funding, arming, or administering Contra programs. He stated that he is not involved with any covert operations being run in the United States."	
Report from F.B.I. interview with Oliver North, July 22, 1986.	

"I've not raised a nickel for the contras."

Oliver North,
public briefing at the
National Security Council
November 7, 1985

"The residual funds from this transaction [with Iran] are allocated as follows: $12 million will be used to purchase critically needed supplies for the Nicaraguan Democratic Resistance Forces. This material is essential to 'bridge' the period between now and when Congressionally-approved lethal assistance can be delivered."

Oliver North,
The 'Diversion Memo',
April 4 & 5, 1986

North

"By fall 1985, Lt. Col. North was actively engaged in private efforts to resupply the contras with lethal equipment.
Evidence suggests that at least by November 1985, Lt. Col. North had assumed a direct operational role, coordinating logistical arrangements to ship privately purchased arms to the Contras."

The Tower Commission Report
February 1987

"In response to specific questions, Ollie covered the following points:
• contact with FDN and UNO aimed to foster viable, democratic, political strategy for Nicaraguan opposition, gave no military advice, knew of no specific military

operations;
• Singlaub--gave no advice,has had no contact in 20 months;
• [Robert] Owen--never worked from OLN [North's] office, OLN had casual contact, never provided Owen guidance."

Oliver North,
Testimony before House Select
Committee on Intelligence
Recounted in an internal NSC
staff account,
October 11, 1986

"The [CIA] field officer testified before the Board: '[T]his private benefactor operation...was, according to my understanding, controlled by Colonel North.' He also informed the Board that all the shipments he was involved in were arms deliveries; 'This was all lethal. Benefactors only sent lethal stuff."

The Tower Commission Report
February, 1987

"Singlaub will be here to see me tomorrow. With your permission, I will ask him to approach [x] at the [Taiwan] Interests Section and [y] at the [South Korean] embassy urging that they proceed with their offer [to aid the contras]."

Oliver North,
Memo to Robert McFarlane,
February 6, 1985

"We don't engage--I mean the State Department's function in this has not been to raise money, other than to try to raise it from Congress. And we do not know where the money was coming from in terms of which individuals were giving it."

Elliot Abrams,
Assistant Secretary of State for
Inter-American Affairs,
before the Senate Select
Committee on Intelligence,
November 25, 1986

"We did not engage in, nor did we really know anything about this private network."
Elliot Abrams,
Feb. 2, 1987

Abrams

"I went down item by item by item, the things that I was doing [to aid the contras], and asked them point blank whether or not I had to continue to do them."
Oliver North,
Recalling a Pentagon meeting attended by Elliot Abrams and Assistant Secretary of Defense Richard Armitage,
before the Joint Select Committee,
July 7, 1987

"Following the conclusion of his 'understanding' with [dissident contra leader Eden] Pastora...and his subsequent conversation with you, [private contra fund-raiser John] Singlaub had worked out with Calero...to supply Pastora's forces inside Nicaragua with a token amount of military equipment...Singlaub tried to raise this with [CIA Director] Bill Casey, who ducked and told Singlaub to take it up with you [Abrams]. Singlaub wants you to try to turn this thing around...we agreed I would call Calero with your answer...I vote for saying yes to Calero...(Comment: The simplest way to handle this would be over the secure phone. NSC approval will be needed, [deleted] will have to be informed.)"
Richard Melton,
Director of the Office on Central America,
State Department,
Memorandum for Elliot Abrams,
May 8, 1986

"If a few hundred rifles were received at a contra camp, the U.S. would know of it promptly. [But] we had no information at any time about who was paying for this." *Elliot Abrams,* *Interview with Washington Post,* *December 12, 1986*	"Mr. Tambs said officials in Washington directed him and the chief of the CIA station in Costa Rica to give logistical help to the contras and to the Americans who were flying weapons and other supplies to the rebels...Asked specifically whom he was referring to, [Tambs] said: "The RIG: Abrams, the guy across the river"-Mr. Fiers, in CIA headquarters in Langley, Virginia- "and North." *New York Times,* *May 3, 1987*
"When asked specifically if he helped devise flight plans for the supply operation, [Col. James] Steele [head of the U.S. Military Group in El Salvador] said: 'My actions were certainly appropriate when I was in El Salvador, and I didn't do anything inappropriate.'" *Philadelphia Inquirer,* *January 18, 1987*	"Steele has fully briefed Ambassador [to El Salvador Edwin Corr] on our ops [operations]... Ambassador very supportive including [weapons] drops [to the contras] such as we have tonight." *Robert Dutton,* *retired Air Force Colonel who supervised the contra resupply operations,* *message to his employer, retired Maj.* *Gen. Richard Secord,* *April 10, 1986*

II. WHO ARE THE CONTRAS?

ISSUE: Has the Reagan Administration consistently misrepresented the real nature of the contras and their backers?

ADMINISTRATION POSITION	COUNTEREVIDENCE
"I have spoken recently of the freedom fighters of Nicaragua...They are the moral equal of our Founding Fathers and the brave men and women of the French Resistance. We cannot turn away from them, for the struggle here is not right versus left, it is right versus wrong." *President Reagan,* *March 1, 1985*	"The FDN is believed to consist of about 800 activists from the following organizations: -- 15 September Legion, military arm of the Nicaraguan Revolutionary Democratic Alliance (ARDEN), a 'Somocista' group founded by [contra military commander Enrique] Bermudez and Herberto Sanchez...[elements that split from the Legion formed] a terrorist group comprised of a small number of commandos believed to be operating out of Honduras" *Weekly Intelligence Summary,* *Prepared by Defense Intelligence Agency,* *July 16, 1982*
"The truth about the democratic resistance is that it is a popular movement led mostly by men who fought in the revolution against Somoza." *George Shultz,* *Secretary of State,* *April 22, 1985*  *Shultz*	"[T]he people [contra leader] Adolfo Calero surrounds himself with are liars and greed and power motivated. They are not the people to rebuild a new Nicaragua. In fact, the FDN has done a good job of keeping competent people out of the organization... In fact, I have probably never been more discouraged...there are few of the so-called leaders of the movement who really care about the boys in the field. THIS WAR HAS BECOME A BUSINESS TO MANY OF [the contras]; THERE

IS STILL A BELIEF THE MA-
RINES ARE GOING TO HAVE
TO INVADE, SO LET'S GET
SET SO WE WILL AUTOMA-
TICALLY BE THE ONES PUT
INTO POWER...
If the $100 million is approved and
things go on as they have these last
five years, it will be like pouring
money down a sink hole."

Robert Owen,
State Department contract employee
Memo to Lt. Col. Oliver North, NSC
Director of Political-Military Affairs,
March 17, 1986

Motley

"The freedom fighters are
peasants, farmers, shopkeepers and vendors. Their leaders are without exception
men who opposed Somoza."

Langhorne Motley,
Assistant Secretary of State for
Inter-American Affairs,
before the House Subcommittee
onWestern Hemisphere Affairs,
January 29, 1985

"In reality, the resistance
leaders are fighting for a return to the principles of democracy, which they be-
lieved had been won in the
triumph over Somoza...The
myth that the resistance
movement is Somoza's Na-
tional Guard attempting to
regain power is perpetuated

by the Sandinistas and their supporters, however. The facts are quite different...Of the 14 Regional Commands of the FDN, three are headed by former National Guardsmen, while six are headed by former Sandinistas."

"The Challenge to Democracy in Central America",
Department of State,
June, 1986

"In contrast to FDN claims about the military leadership of the contras, 46 of the 48 positions in the FDN military leadership are held by ex-National Guardsmen. These include the Strategic Commander, the Regional Command Coordinator, all five members of the General Staff, four out of five Central Commanders, five out of six regional commanders, and all 30 task force commanders."

"Who are the Contras",
Report of the Congressional Arms Control and Foreign Policy Caucus,
April 18, 1985

"The contra army remains a peasant army commanded by former National Guardsmen...12 of the 13 members of the FDN's *Estado Mayor* -- the Military High Command or, literally, the 'Chiefs of Staff' -- are today, as they have been since 1980, ex-National Guard officers."

"The Contra High Command: An Independent Analysis of the Military Leadership of the FDN",
Report of the Congressional Arms Control and Foreign Policy Caucus,
March, 1986

ADMINISTRATION POSITION	COUNTEREVIDENCE
"UNO [United Nicaraguan Opposition] has further strengthened unity by ensuring that all its military forces are responsive to its civilian leadership." *Presidential Message to Congress, March, 1986*	"I put it as FDN/UNO because FDN is now driving UNO, not the other way around. UNO is a creation of the USG [US Government] to garner support from Congress. When it was founded a year ago, the hope was it would become a viable organization. In fact, almost anything it has accomplished is because the hand of the USG has been there directing and manipulating... But, if USG agencies actually believe that UNO is a strong and functioning body that truly represents all factions of the Democratic Resistance, they are fooling themselves into believing something that is not true..." *Robert Owen,* *Memo to Oliver North,* *March 17, 1986*
"The ulitimate distortion ...speaks of the Agency 'having to be stopped for illegal ...murders.' This distortion of reality must be corrected." *William J. Casey,* *Director of the CIA,* *Letter to members of the Senate and House Intelligence Committees, in response to revelation of the CIA assassination manual for the contras,* *October 25, 1984*	

"It is possible to neutralize carefully selected and planned targets, such as court judges, mesta judges, police and state security officials... professional criminals will be hired to carry out specific selective 'jobs'."

"Psychological Operations and Guerrilla Warfare",
CIA manual for Nicaraguan contras,
Fall, 1983

Casey

"[I]t was standard FDN practice to kill prisoners and suspected Sandinista collaborators. In talking with officers in FDN camps I frequently heard offhand remarks like, "Oh, I cut his throat." The CIA did not discourage such tactics. To the contrary, the Agency severely criticized me when I admitted to the press that the FDN had regularly kidnapped and executed agrarian reform workers and civilians. We were told that the only way to defeat the Sandinistas was to use the tactics [that] the Agency attributed to 'communist' insurgencies elsewhere: kill, kidnap, rob and torture."

Edgar Chamorro,
a former Director of the Nicaraguan Democratic Force (FDN),
excerpt from affadavit testimony before the International Court of Justice,
signed September 5, 1985

"'[Contra] incidents' during this

period [1982] involved...attacks by small guerrilla bands on individual Sandinista soldiers and the assassination of minor government officials and a Cuban advisor."'
Weekly Intelligence Summary, Prepared by the Defense Intelligence Agency, July 16, 1982

"The principal point which should be made is that there is nobody in the FDN who is there against his/her will-- it is an entirely voluntary organization."
Comment of Nicaraguan Democratic Force (FDN) Panel on the Brody Report, Central Intelligence Agency, January 30, 1986

"The contras also engage in widespread kidnapping of civilians, apparently for the purposes of recruitment as well as intimidation."
Aryeh Neier, Vice-Chairman of Americas Watch, in New York Times, February 10, 1987

"Leaders of the resistance are aware that their forces must follow a high standard of conduct...A guerilla movement guilty of widespread abuse would not be attracting thousands of young men and women to join its cause."
"The Challenge to Democracy in Central America", Department of State, October, 1986

"During 1986 a major human rights problem was widespread and continuing violation of the laws of war regarding treatment of civilians by the contra forces. The leadership of the contra organizations has taken no meaningful steps to investigate and punish these abuses, which range from indiscriminate and often fatal attacks on civilians to selective murder, mistreatment and kidnapping. A significant number of kidnap victims are children."
"Human Rights in Nicaragua", Americas Watch report, February, 1987

III. THE REAGAN RECORD ON PEACE NEGOTIATIONS

ISSUE: Has the Reagan Administration supported a negotiated peace settlement for the conflicts in Central America, particularly the U.S. war against Nicaragua, by backing the Contadora and other regional peace initiatives, as it has claimed publicly?

ADMINISTRATION POSITION	COUNTEREVIDENCE
"The administration has always supported regional diplomatic initiatives aimed at peace and democracy, whether it be through Contadora, through face-to-face meetings with the ruling party in Nicaragua or through current Central American initiatives." *President Reagan,* *Speech before the American* *Newspaper Publishers'* *Association,* *May 3, 1987*	"Continue active negotiations but agree on no treaty and agree to work out some way to support the Contras either directly or indirectly. Withhold true objectives from staffs." *John Poindexter,* *Deputy National Security Advisor,* *memo to Robert McFarlane,* *National Security Advisor* *November 23, 1984*

Reagan

"We have trumped the latest Nicaraguan/Mexican efforts to rush signature of an unsatisfactory Contadora agreement...the situation remains fluid and requires careful management...
"We have effectively blocked Contadora group efforts to impose the second draft of the Revised Contadora Act."

Background paper for National Security Council meeting on Central America, October 30, 1984

"Prepare a 'Dear Colleague' letter for signature by a responsible Democrat which counsels against 'negotiating' with the FSLN."

Lt. Col. Oliver North ,
NSC Director of Political-Military Affairs,
Memo to Robert McFarlane
March 20, 1985

"[T]he substance of the 21 Contadora objectives is virtually identical with our own evaluation of what is necessary to satisfy U.S. interests in the area...We support the Contadora process."

Elliot Abrams,
Assistant Secretary for Inter-American Affairs,
Testimony before the Senate Committee on Foreign Relations
February 5, 1987

"We are committed to the Nicaraguan resistance. Our support will not slacken whatever the results in Contadora."

Elliot Abrams,
Memo to Richard H. Melton, Director of the Office on Central America, State Department,
May 22, 1986

"We are afraid that it [the Contadora group] will pressure the U.S. and friends to accept an agreement rather than a good agreement. Collapse would be better than a bad agreement...We need to develop an active diplomacy now to head off efforts at Latin Solidarity aimed against the U.S. and our allies."

Elliot Abrams,
memo to U.S. Chiefs of Mission Conference held in Panama,
September 8-10, 1985

Abrams

ADMINISTRATION POSITION	COUNTEREVIDENCE
"The United States has remained constant in its support for a comprehensive, verifiable and simultaneous implementation of the 21 objectives agreed on by all countries in the Contadora peace process." *George Shultz,* *Secretary of State,* *Speech before the American Bar Association,* *February 12, 1987*	"If we can continue to fund the contras (or, if necessary, alternative benefactors are found), negotiations can proceed at a measured pace with the U.S. in the background." *George Shultz,* *Memo to the President,* *September 6, 1983*
"United States support of regional diplomatic peace efforts has been strong and consistent, and it continues undiminished." *"Resource Book: The Contadora Process",* *U.S. Department of State,* *January, 1985*	"Contadora negotiations are scheduled to resume in Panama on Friday, May 16. [deleted] the Sandinistas will likely proclaim that they are prepared to sign another version of the treaty...We will then find ourselves engaged in a propaganda contest in which each side will claim the other is intransigent. Our objective should be to support our friends' position as a positive and constructive Central American effort to deal with the region's problems, while denouncing the Sandinistas for refusing to negotiate." *John Poindexter,* *National Security Advisor* *Memo for the National Security Planning Group* *May 15, 1986*

IV. THE ROLE OF PRESIDENT REAGAN AND VICE PRESIDENT BUSH

ISSUE: Between October 1984 and October 1986, the United States Congress enacted the Boland Amendment, which banned the Reagan Administration from providing direct or indirect support for military or paramilitary activities against the government of Nicaragua. Did President Reagan know of, approve, or assist efforts by members of his Administration to secretly raise funds to militarily support the Nicaraguan contras during this period?

ADMINISTRATION POSITION	COUNTEREVIDENCE
"The president told the [Tower] Board on January 26, 1987, that he did not know that the NSC staff was engaged in helping the contras." *The Tower Commission Report* *February 26, 1987*	"*Q:* ...Did you ever give the president reports on what you and your staff were doing to carry out his wishes [to aid the contras after U.S. funding was cut off]? *A:* Frequently, yes sir. *Q:* On how many occasions? *A:* Dozens.*" *Robert McFarlane,* *former National Security Advisor* *before the Joint Select Committee,* *May 13, 1987*

Reagan

"*Q:* Well, if I were to read this to you: 'The President told the Board on January 26, 1987 that he did not know that the NSC staff was engaged in helping the contras'...does that come as a surprise to you? *North:* Yes."

Lt. Col. Oliver North,
NSC Director of Political-Military
Affairs, before the Joint Select
Committee,
July 9, 1987

ADMINISTRATION POSITION	COUNTEREVIDENCE
"I'm kind of a stranger to this whole thing. I didn't know anything about it. I was told they [contra benefactors who visited Reagan] were raising money to pay for TV ads...I didn't know they had a foundation or anything else." *President Reagan,* *April 30, 1987*	"President Reagan...hosted White House briefings for private citizens who donated millions of dollars used to buy weapons for Nicaraguan rebels, ABC News reported last night. Records show that about $2.2 million was contributed to a [contra fund-raiser 'Spitz'] Channell project code-named 'Toys', and that the money was used for military aid to the contras at a time when Congress had barred such assistance, ABC said." *Washington Post,* *February 13, 1987* "Reagan wrote at least four letters to Channell praising either NEPL [National Endowment for the Preservation of Liberty] or Channell's political action committee, the American Conservative Trust." *Washington Post,* *May 1, 1987*
"I don't know how that money was to be used. I have no knowledge that there was ever any solicitation by our people with those people [private contra donors]." *President Reagan* *May 5, 1987*	"I was aware that the president was aware of third country support, that the president was aware of private support [to the contras]." *John Poindexter,* *National Security Advisor,* *before the Joint Select Committee,* *July 15, 1987*

ADMINISTRATION POSITION	COUNTEREVIDENCE
"...we've been aware that there are private groups and private citizens that have been trying to help the contras, to that extent, but we don't know the exact particulars of what they're doing." *President Reagan,* *October 8, 1986*	"...Information regarding the [Saudi] prince's expressed interest in donating to the Nicaraguan Freedom Fighters was discussed by North personally with President Reagan and National Security Advisor McFarlane as recently as June, 1985." *FBI Cable from Washington Field Office* *to Director of FBI,* *July 28, 1985* "Now the contra situation...there's no question about my being informed. I've known what's going on there, as a matter of fact, for quite a long time now, a matter of years...And to suggest that I am just finding out or that things are being exposed that I didn't know about -- no. Yes, I was kept briefed on that....As a matter of fact, I was very definitely involved in the decisions about support to the freedom fighters--my idea to begin with." *President Reagan,* *White House briefing,* *May 15, 1987*
"Another country was facilitating those sales of weapons systems [to Iran]. They then were overcharging and were apparently putting money into bank accounts of the leaders of the contras. It wasn't us funneling money to them. This was another country." *President Reagan,* *Interview with Time Magazine,* *December 8, 1986*	"The residual funds from the [Iranian arms] transaction are allocated as follows:...$12 million will be used to purchase critically needed supplies for the Nicaraguan Resistance Forces....Recommendation: that the president approve the structure depicted above." *Oliver North,* *Memo to John Poindexter, to be forwarded to President Reagan,* *April, 1986*

ISSUE: Were Vice-President George Bush and members of his staff aware of the secret contra resupply effort before it was publicly disclosed by Attorney General Edwin Meese on November 25, 1986? Specifically, did the Vice-President or his staff know of, approve, or assist Felix Rodriguez's (alias Max Gomez) role in the contra supply program while Rodriguez was based in El Salvador?

ADMINISTRATION POSITION	COUNTEREVIDENCE
"On the three occasions when the vice president met with Mr. Rodriguez, the discussions dealt entirely with the insurgency in El Salvador and there was no discussion, direct or indirect, of the contra aid network... There was no mention of supply or support operations for the contras whatsoever." *Statement by the Office of Vice President George Bush, December 15, 1986*	"Briefing Memorandum for the Vice President Event: Meeting with Felix Rodriguez Date: Thursday, May 1, 1986 Time: 11:30 - 11:45 am, West Wing [of White House] From: Don Gregg I. PURPOSE Felix Rodriguez, a counterinsurgency expert who is visiting from El Salvador, will provide a briefing on the status of the war in El Salvador and **resupply of the contras.**" [emphasis added] *Briefing memorandum dated April 30, 1986 for May 1 meeting between Vice President Bush and Felix Rodriguez, Oliver North and U.S. Ambassador to El Salvador Edwin Corr*

Bush

"Felix [Rodriguez] talking too much about V[ice] P[resident] connection."
Oliver North, handwritten notes, January 9, 1986

ADMINISTRATION POSITION	COUNTEREVIDENCE
"There is this insidious suggestion that I was conducting an operation. It's untrue, unfair, and totally wrong. I met Max Gomez three times and never discussed Nicaragua with him ...There was no linkage to any operation, yet it keeps coming up. There are all kinds of weirdos coming out of the woodwork on this thing." *George Bush,* *Interview with Time Magazine* *January 26, 1987*	"I have just met here with Felix Rodriguez...he is operating as a private citizen, but his acquaintanceship with the VP [Vice-President] is real enough, going back to latter's days as DCI [Director of Central Intelligence]. Rodriguez' **primary commitment** [emphasis added] to the region is in [deleted] where he wants to assist the FDN [the major contra grouping]. I told him that the FDN deserved his priority." *Gen. Paul Gorman,* *Commander of the U.S. Southern Command,* *Cable to U.S. Ambassador to El Salvador Thomas Pickering and Col. James Steele,* *February 14, 1985*
"[Donald] Gregg has said he had no knowledge of anything involving contras... Neither the Vice President nor anyone on his staff is directly or indirectly coordinating an operation in Central America." *Marlin Fitzwater,* *Spokesperson for Vice-President Bush* *New York Times* *October 13, 1986*	"Felix Rodriguez indicated on August 8, 1986, in a meeting with Don Gregg that he had knowledge of the contra aid network which he wanted to discuss with U.S. officials...On November 7, 1986, Mr Rodriguez met with Mr. Gregg and Colonel Watson in Gregg's office...Mr. Rodriguez also indicated that he, himself, had been able to assist the Contra resupply effort." *Office of the Vice President,* *December 15, 1986* *Statement by the Press Secretary,*
"The only thing that I talked to Max about was his involvement in the insurgency in El Salvador." *Donald Gregg,* *National Security Advisor to Vice President Bush,* *CBS Evening News* *December 16, 1986*	"A swap of weapons for $ was arranged to get aid for the contras. [Thomas] Clines and Secord tied in." *Donald Gregg,* *in hand-written notes from meeting with Felix Rodriguez,* *August 8, 1986*

V. MISUSE OF HUMANITARIAN AID

ISSUE: In 1985, Congress approved $27 million in aid to the contras for 'humanitarian' aid. In so doing, Congress retained the prohibitions on lethal assistance in the Boland Amendment. Did Reagan officials violate the law by misusing these funds for other than humanitarian purposes? Has the administration fully accounted for the disbursement of the $27 million?

ADMINISTRATION POSITION	COUNTEREVIDENCE
"We believe that the NHAO [Nicaraguan Humanitarian Affairs Office] established adequate procedures as required by law, and that there was in fact no significant diversion of U.S. assistance provided under this program from authorized purposes." *Robert W. Duemling,* *Director of the State* *Department's Nicaraguan* *Humanitarian Affair's Office,* *Letter to Frank Conahan,* *Government Accounting Office* *October 23, 1986*	"A GAO [General Accounting Office] investigation alleged, and the Fraud Section's investigation confirmed, that large amounts of money paid by the NHAO, set up to administer the twenty seven million dollars appropriated to fund humanitarian aid to the contras, cannot be accounted for. Some of the funds that have been traced ended up in secret accounts in the Caymans or were apparently used to bribe members of the Honduran military. Although there are receipts showing that the contras actually received the humanitarian aid allegedly purchased, it has so far not been determined if many of these receipts are genuine (many are signed with false names), and some have been conclusively demonstrated to be fraudulent...The fraud section has conclusively established that some of the money appropriated for humanitarian aid was used to buy weapons, an act clearly prohibited by the Boland Amendment. This act involved the submission of false

McFarlane

documentation to the US government and was committed by 'unilateral assets' of the CIA."

Ralph Martin,
Deputy Assistant Attorney General,
Memo to William Weld, Assistant
Attorney General,
November 27, 1986

"Recent contacts with the resistance have focused on ensuring that the $27 million in humanitarian assistance is properly administered and fully compliant with the legal requirements contained in the legislation....we agree on the desirability of this outcome and that it must be achieved within the limits of our law."

Robert McFarlane,
National Security Advisor,
Letter to Rep. Michael Barnes,
Chairman, House Subcommittee
on Western Hemisphere Affairs,
September 12, 1985

"NHAO visited the region in June 1986 and found that it had paid about $80,000 based on false receipts. Some funds were used to purchase ammunition and grenades."

"Central America: Problems in
Controlling Funds for the Nicaraguan
Democratic Resistance",
General Accounting Office Report,
December, 1986

"*Q:* Are you satisfied that there will be ample accountability?
Motley: There will be ample scrutiny, I am satisfied of that. We will do every-

thing we can to stick to the letter of the law."

Langhorne Motley,
Assistant Secretary of State for
Inter-American Affairs,
before the Senate Committee on
Appropriations,
April 18, 1985

"NHAO was the worst possible vehicle which could have been devised to pay the bills. Because there is no verification it is impossible to ensure the integrity to the operation."

Robert Owen,
State Dept. contract employee with
NHAO,
Memo to Lt. Col. Oliver North,
March 17, 1986

"NHAO has in place a system regulating the scrutiny of assistance requests and personnel contracts, and payment disbursed to authorized suppliers. These procedures further enable NHAO to exercise oversight responsibility to ensure the observance of legislative guidelines concerning the use of assistance."

Elliot Abrams,
Assistant Secretary of State for
Inter-American Affairs
before the House Subcommittee
on Western Hemisphere Affairs,
December 5, 1985

"Elliot Abrams, the administration's man in charge of the 'contra' war, kept government auditors from verifying that none of the $27 million in U.S. humanitarian aid to Nicaraguan rebels was spent for weapons, administration officials disclosed yesterday...A senior GAO official said it was impossible to tell whether the diversion of funds for arms was an isolated incident or was part of a general pattern because GAO auditors were prevented by Mr. Abrams... [from] going to Central America to see for themselves."

Baltimore Sun,
December 7, 1986

Abrams

"One contra witness informed the fraud section that the head of the NHAO (who reported directly to Assistant Secretary Abrams) instructed him to certify that humanitarian aid had been received after the witness informed the

Ambassador that he had no such information....The press has reported that records of the Salvadorean telephone company show conclusively that calls were made from safe houses used in the airdrops of weapons to the contras, to a contractor associated with the NHAO ...According to the press, witnesses have stated that there were large quantities of munitions aboard the NHAO's supposedly humanitarian airdrops into Nicaragua."

Department of Justice memo from Ralph Martin to William Weld, November 27, 1986

"I am convinced that the $27 million went for the purposes intended and the people intended."

Robert Duemling, Director of NHAO, New York Times, December 4, 1986

"Robert Duemling, director of the State Department agency that administered the $27 million humanitarian aid program, said this week that although he opposed putting weapons aboard the humanitarian aid cargo planes, he authorized at least two mixed loads on instruction from [Elliot] Abrams' office."

Miami Herald August 14, 1987

"According to sources who spoke with Senator Kerry's staff, one of [Francisco 'Paco'] Chanes' business partners or close associates is alleged to be Frank Castro, an unindicted co-conspirator in the Fernandez Marijuana Smuggling Syndicate case, in which the principals in the narcotics ring secretly bought a South Florida commercial bank, Sunshine Bank, with drug profits. Chanes is one of three persons who controls the broker account of Frigorificos de Puntarennas, a company which received $231,587 in official 'humanitarian' funds from NHAO."

"Private Assistance and the Contras: A Staff Report",
Senator John Kerry,
October 14, 1986

"I can testify that we have regular reporting on deliveries made in theater and that no one has ever complained about the failure to pay or the failure to deliver."

Elliot Abrams
before the House Subcommittee on Western Hemisphere Affairs March 5, 1986

"A corner grocery supplying Nicaraguan Contra rebels at American expense billed the U.S. government for thousands of uniforms that never existed, reliable sources say. The sources say the Supermercado Hermano Pedro is also a front to disguise the participation of several Honduran military officers in Contra supply efforts while Honduran public records and officials say the grocery store has hidden at least $3.6 million in U.S. payments from Honduran tax authorities..."

Miami Herald
May 9, 1986

VI. THE CONTRA/DRUG CONNECTION

ISSUE: Have the Nicaraguan contras been involved in smuggling drugs--particularly cocaine--into the United States? Were members of the Reagan Administration aware of such activity by the contras and their supporters?

ADMINISTRATION POSITION	COUNTEREVIDENCE
"[T]here has been no evidence that organizations associated with the major resistance umbrella group [the United Nicaraguan Opposition] have participated or benefitted from drug trafficking." *"Allegations of Drug Trafficking in the Nicaraguan Democratic Resistance",* *Department of State,* *July, 1986*	"DC-6 which is being used for runs [to supply the contras] out of New Orleans is probably being used for drug runs into U.S." *Lt. Col. Oliver North,* *NSC Director of Political-Military* *Affairs, handwritten notes from meeting* *with Robert Owen, State Department* *contract employee,* *August 9, 1985* "People who are questionable [in the contra movement] because of past indiscretions [sic] include: Jose Robelo (Chepon): potential involvement with drug running...Sebastian Gonzalez (Wachan): Now involved in drug running out of Panama." *Robert Owen,* *Memo to Oliver North,* *April 1, 1985* "No doubt you know the DC-4 Foley got was used at one time to run drugs, and part of the crew had criminal records. Nice group the boys [the CIA] choose." *Robert Owen,* *Memo to Oliver North,* *February 10, 1986*

"I have talked to the DEA [Drug Enforcement Agency] and there is absolutely no evidence, nor any accusation of any involvement with drugs by the FDN [The Nicaraguan Democratic Force, the principal contra grouping]."

Elliot Abrams,
Assistant Secretary of State for
Inter-American Affairs,
before the House Subcommittee
on Western Hemisphere Affairs,
March 6, 1986

Abrams

"Officials from several [U.S. government] agencies said that by early last fall [1986] the Drug Enforcement Administration office in Guatemala had compiled convincing evidence that the contra military supply operation was smuggling cocaine and marijuana."

New York Times,
January 20, 1987

"I believe that there is no question, based on things we have heard, that contras and the contra infrastructure have been involved in the cocaine trade and in bringing cocaine into Florida ."

Jack Blum,
Special Counsel to the Senate Committee
on Foreign Relations,
Los Angeles Times
Feb 18, 1987

"[A]llegations have been circulating regarding Nicaraguan Democratic Resistance participation in drug trafficking. The administration believes these allegations are false."

J. Edward Fox,
Assistant Secretary of State for
Legislative and Intergovernmental
Affairs,
in letter to Congress,
July 24, 1986

"Chairman Kerry: [D]id you make some agreement about running guns down to various locations and bringing drugs back?
Mr. Morales: Yes, I did. That was part of the agreement.
Chairman Kerry: Where was the money coming from?
Mr. Morales: Drugs.
Chairman Kerry: Did they [the contras] know that?
Mr. Morales: Of course they knew that....They were their own

drugs.

Chairman Kerry: Whose drugs?

Mr. Morales: The contra drugs.

Chairman Kerry: How do you know they were contra drugs?

Mr. Morales: They told me..."

George Morales,
pilot who flew drugs and weapons to the contras,
before the Security and Terrorism Subcommittee of the Senate Foreign Relations Committee,
July 15, 1987

"[George] Morales, who provided the planes, and [Gary] Betzner, who flew them, both claim that CIA agents and other U.S. officials helped the contras run the drugs-out, guns-in operation. 'I smuggled my share of illegal substance,' said Betzner, 'but I also smuggled my share of weapons in exchange, with the full knowledge and assistance of both the DEA [Drug Enforcement Agency] and the CIA.'"

Newsweek
January 26, 1986

ISSUE: Has the Reagan Administration misrepresented its case that the Nicaraguan government is involved in drug trafficking?

ADMINISTRATION POSITION	COUNTEREVIDENCE
"Every American parent will be outraged to learn that top Nicaraguan government	"The Drug Enforcement Administration today disputed an assertion by President Reagan. In a state-

ADMINISTRATION POSITION	COUNTEREVIDENCE
officials are deeply involved in drug trafficking." *President Reagan,* *in nationally televised speech,* *March 16, 1986*	ment, the Drug Enforcement Administration, which is the principal agency in drug-smuggling investigations, said it had no information implicating "the Minister of Interior or other Nicaraguan officials [in drug trafficking]." *New York Times* *March 19, 1986*
"[T]here is incontrovertible proof that the Nicaraguan government has participated in drug-trafficking." *George Shultz,* *Secretary of State,* *before the Senate Committee on Foreign Relations,* *February 27, 1986*	"We do not believe that Nicaragua is a drug source country..." *Thomas G. Byrne,* *Deputy Assistant Administrator for Intelligence, Drug Enforcement Administration,* *before the House Committee on Foreign Affairs,* *March 11, 1986*

VII. ADMINISTRATION SOLICITATION OF THIRD COUNTRY AID TO THE CONTRAS

ISSUE: Did Reagan Administration officials solicit other countries to provide funding or arms to the contras, which was contrary to the intent of the Boland Amendment?

ADMINISTRATION POSITION	COUNTEREVIDENCE
"[T]here is a prohibition against any U.S. assistance whether direct or indirect which to us would infer also soliciting and/or encouraging third countries; and we have refrained from doing that...We are going to continue to comply with the law. I am not looking for any loopholes...And that is pretty plain English; it does not have to be written by any bright, young lawyers. And we are going to continue to comply with that." *Langhorne Motley,* *Assistant Secretary of State for* *Inter-American Affairs,* *before the Senate Foreign* *Relations Committee,* *March 26, 1985*	"Singlaub will be here to see me tomorrow. With your permission, I will ask him to approach [X] at the [Taiwan] Interests Section and [Y] at the [South Korean] Embassy urging that they proceed with their offer [to aid the contras]." *Lt. Col. Oliver North,* *NSC Director for Political-Military* *Affairs* *Memo to Robert McFarlane,* *February 6, 1985*

Motley

ADMINISTRATION POSITION	COUNTEREVIDENCE
"It is equally important to stress what we did not do. We did not solicit funds or other support for military or paramilitary activities either from Americans or third parties." *Robert McFarlane,* *National Security Advisor,* *Letter to Rep. Lee Hamilton,* *Chairman, House Select* *Committee on Intelligence,* *September 5, 1985*	"In May, 1984 a foreign national offered to contribute to the support of the Contras. I did not solicit the offer and when it was made, I should have told him to direct his interest to Contra representatives. I did not, and instead, learned where he should send his contribution in this country and so informed him... I would estimate it may have come to as much as $5 million." *Robert McFarlane* *Letter to Rep. Lee Hamilton,* *February 8, 1987*
"*McFarlane:* I did not solicit any country at any time to make contributions to the contras.I have seen the reports that various have, [deeted] third countries, and I have no idea of the extent of that or anything else... *Q:* Were you aware of the efforts of other members of the administration in these solicitations? *McFarlane:* Well, I am not, and only in the stories in the last two days have I seen this report about what happened after, I take it, it became a legal matter, to once more do so." *Robert McFarlane* *House Committee on Foreign Affairs,* *December 8, 1986*	"April 16, 1984: McFARLANE proposes seeking support for Nicaraguan opposition from country #1 [Israel] in a discussion with GSP [Secretary of State George Shultz], [CIA Director] CASEY and two State officials... May 23, 1984:...McFARLANE advised Ambassador to [Israel Samuel Lewis] that he had dropped his idea that country #1 take over all responsibility for the Nicaraguan opposition forces because Ambassador 'blew the whistle on him'." *Testimony of George Shultz,* *Secretary of State,* *Chronology of Non-USG [U.S. Government] Support for the Nicaraguan Opposition,* *July 23, 1987*

ADMINISTRATION POSITION	COUNTEREVIDENCE
"The Senate Intelligence Committee aide said Thursday that the CIA has said flatly that the Saudi Government is not funding the contras." *Los Angeles Times,* *October 10, 1986*	"June 16, 1986: McFarlane advises GPS [Secretary of State George Shultz] that Country 2 [Saudi Arabia] volunteered and delivered $31 million to the Nicaraguan opposition while USG aid was barred." *Testimony of George Shultz,* *Chronology of Non-USG Support for* *Nicaraguan Opposition.* *July 23, 1987*
"I think that I can say that while I have been Assistant Secretary, which is about 15 months, we [the US government] have not received a dime from a foreign government, not a dime, from any foreign government [for the contras]." *Elliot Abrams,* *Assistant Secretary of State for* *Inter-American Affairs,* *before the Senate Committee on* *Foreign Relations* *October 10, 1986*	"Singlaub....plans to seek funds ($10 million) from these governments [South Korea and Taiwan] ...He will be looking for us to give the nod [deleted] at the appropriate moment. For now, he would like us to inform the [deleted] Singlaub will be there [deleted] 'on a mission which is in keeping with the policy of the Administration' or some such." *Richard H. Melton,* *Director of the Office of Central American* *Affairs, State Department,* *Memo to Elliot Abrams,* *May 8, 1986*
"With respect to private solicitations, we never did any of that. We in the [State] department never made any other solicitation for anything from anyone...We had virtually no, we had no information on who was paying for it...We did not engage in nor did we really know anything about this private network." *Elliot Abrams,* *The Tower Commission Report,* *February, 1987*	"He [Elliot Abrams] said he had recommended Brunei where Shultz is going to visit. They have lots of money and very little to spend it on. It seems like a good prospect. Shultz agrees. I asked Elliot how the money could be transferred. He said he thought Shultz could just hand them an account number." *John Poindexter,* *National Security Advisor,* *Message to Oliver North,* *June 11, 1986*

"The Chairman: Do you know if any foreign government is helping to supply the contras? *Mr. George:* No sir, we have no intelligence of that."

Clair George,
CIA Director of Operations,
before the House Select
Committee on Intelligence,
October 14, 1986

Abrams

"We don't engage -- I mean the State Department's function in this has not been to raise money, other than to try to raise it from the Congress....And we did not know where the money was coming from in terms of which individuals were giving it."

Elliot Abrams,
before the Senate Select
Committee on Intelligence,
November 25, 1986

"August 6, 1986: Abrams reports that he will be meeting an official of Brunei. Reports also that he has received a second account number from the CIA."

Testimony of George Shultz,
Chronology of Non-USG support for
Nicaraguan Opposition
July 23, 1987

Q: Mr. McMahon, these are the cables that I showed you before the deposition, correct?
A: Right.
Q: And in general terms they describe a proposed trip, which did take place, where [Dewey Claridge] went to [South Africa] to discuss the possibility of obtaining aid [deleted] for the contras....
A: That's my recollection of it."

John McMahon,
Former Deputy Director of the CIA,
before the Joint Select Committee,
referring to CIA Director William Casey's
approval to solicit the South African
government for aid to the contras,
June 1, 1987

"October 8-15, 1985: GPS [George Shultz] asks senior official of Country 8 [Singapore] if his government would be willing to supply the [long range] radios [to the contras].
May 16, 1986: NSPG meeting. Discussion of bridge funding for the NDR [Nicaraguan Democratic Resistance] and possible Third Country solicitation for humanitarian assistance. GPS [George Shultz] tasked to draw up list of possible donors. Casey mentions that

Countries 1 [Israel], 2 [Saudi Arabia], 3 [Taiwan] and 5 [South Korea] all have some interest."

Testimony of George Shultz,
Chronology of Non-USG Support for
Nicaraguan Opposition
July 23, 1987

Shultz

"I had no discussion of this matter [contributions to the contras] with the Sultan or anyone else in Brunei."

George Shultz,
before the House Foreign Affairs
Committee,
December 8, 1986

"The donation was made at the request of the US Secretary of State, Mr. George Shultz, in the summer 1986."

Statement by Brunei officials
January 16, 1987

VIII. PRESSURING COSTA RICA

ISSUE: Did Reagan officials put pressure on the Costa Rican government to allow the contras to create a "southern front" in northern Costa Rica to wage war against the Nicaraguan government?

ADMINISTRATION POSITION	COUNTEREVIDENCE
"If there's anybody in the Costa Rican government who is claiming that we are using economic pressure it's false...There have been a lot of extraordinary accusations to defeat the contra aid bill, and this is one of the fairly detestable ones." *Elliot Abrams,* *Assistant Secretary of State for* *Inter-American Affairs,* *Washington Post,* *April 13 ,1986*	"Last night... our Project Democracy rep. in Costa Rica called to advise that the Arias Govt...is going to hold a press conference today...announcing that an illegal support operation for the Contras had been taking place from an airfield from Costa Rica for over a year...I then had a conference call w/ Tambs, Abrams, and [deleted], and we agreed on the following sequence: --North to call Pres. Arias and tell him that if the press conference were held, Arias... would never see a nickel of the $80M [million] that McPherson [head of the Agency for International Development] had promised him earlier on Friday...Arias then got the same word from Elliot... Arias called back to advise that there would be no press conference and no team of reporters sent to the airfield." *Lt. Col. Oliver North,* *NSC Director of Political-Military Affairs,* *note to John Poindexter, National Security Advisor* *September 2, 1986*

North

"No U.S. Government funds were allocated or used in connection with this site [Santa Elena airstrip in northern Costa Rica] nor were any U.S. Government personnel involved in its construction...The Government of Costa Rica has made clear its position that it will not permit the use of its territory for military action against neighboring states. The U.S. Government respects that position."

State Department Press Guidance regarding airstrip in Costa Rica September 30, 1986

"[T]he airstrip at Santa Elena, Costa Rica...was divulged by the Costa Rican Security Minister at a press conference...September 26...The press guidance at Tab I has been coordinated with State (Abrams), Defense (Armitage), and CIA...The damage done by this revelation is considerable...The airfield at Santa Elena has been a vital element in supporting the resistance. Built by a Project Democracy proprietary (Udall Corporation, S.A.-- a Panamanian company), the field was initially used for direct resupply efforts (July 1985-February 1986)...The Arias Administration revelations [have] resulted in the loss of a facility important to keeping the resistance supplied and in the field against the Sandinistas."

Oliver North memorandum for John Poindexter, September 30, 1986

"My understanding was nobody ever used the airstrip, that it had never quite gotten into operation."

Elliot Abrams, before the Tower Commission, February 1987

"The runway was in fact a secret airfield in Costa Rica. LtCol North indicated in a memorandum dated September 30, 1986, that the airfield was used for direct resupply of the Contras from July, 1985 to February, 1986."

The Tower Commission Report, February, 1987

"As far as efforts to intimidate people, I don't believe in that and would not be part of it...We don't take the view with them [Costa Rican officials] that 'unless you do thus and so with the Contras, we're going to cut off your aid."

George Shultz,
Secretary of State,
before the House Subcommittee
on Western Hemisphere Affairs,
March 17, 1986

Shultz

"No US-appropriated funds have been disbursed to Costa Rica during the past six months. A [US] embassy official puts the amount withheld at $85 million, while Costa Rican and US Congressional officials say the total is $140 million."

The Nation,
September 12, 1987

"[I]t is impossible to avoid the suspicion that Costa Rica's 'less favored nation treatment' [by the Reagan Administration] is a form of revenge for having the temerity to disagree with us about the contras."

Francis McNeil,
Former U.S. Ambassador to Costa Rica,
before the House Subcommittee on
Western Hemisphere Affairs,
July 7, 1987

IX. THE HASENFUS AFFAIR

ISSUE: Did the Reagan Administration or the U.S. government have any official connection to the C123 cargo plane shot down over Nicaragua on October 5, 1986, leading to the capture of ex-CIA cargo handler Eugene Hasenfus?

ADMINISTRATION POSITION

"*Q:* Mr. President, was there any U.S. involvement in this flight over Nicaragua, carrying the arms, any involvement whatsoever?
A: I'm glad you asked that. Absolutely not."

President Reagan
October 7, 1986

COUNTEREVIDENCE

"Cooper, Sawyer and Hasenfus with a talker on board departed Ilopango 0950L. Full fuel and 10K lbs ammo. Route same as usual. "

Robert Dutton,
Retired Air Force Colonel, supervised
contra resupply operation,
cable to Lt. Col. Oliver North,
October 6, 1986

"*Q:* ...And what were your duties in connection with this resupply operation to support the contras?
Dutton: I was asked to manage the operation...
Q: ...Who commanded the operation, sir?
Dutton: General Secord and Col. North.
Q: Col. Dutton, on October 5, 1986, what occurred to one of your flights?
Dutton: One of the C123 flights [carrying Hasenfus] was shot down over Nicaragua.
Q: Did you notify Col North's office of that?
Dutton: Yes, I did."

Robert Dutton,
before the Joint Select Committee,
May 27, 1987

ADMINISTRATION POSITION	COUNTEREVIDENCE
"Bush's National Security Advisor [Donald Gregg], was asked yesterday if [Max] Gomez [aka Felix Rodriguez] had called with information on the plane the Sandinistas shot down [carrying Eugene Hasenfus]. *Donald Gregg:* Not directly at all, no. *Q:* But he contacted someone who worked for you? *Gregg:* No." *CBS Evening News Dec. 16, 1986*	"On October 5 and 6, 1986 Mr. [Felix] Rodriguez called twice to say that he had received information that one of the contra resupply aircraft was missing, possibly in Nicaragua." *Chronology released by the office of Vice-President Bush, December 15, 1986* "Sorry Max [Felix Rodriguez] got into this we don't need info or misinfo[rmation] flowing from top down [from Bush's office]...This type situation precisely why I wanted to fly 2-ship...V[ice] P[resident]'s office should know our friend Max is prime reason we have had to send a/c [aircraft] in single. He should be taken out of this net[work]." *Robert Dutton, Message to Oliver North following the downing of the Hasenfus plane October 6, 1986*
"*Evans:* Mr. Secretary, can you give me categorical assurance that Hasenfus was not under the control, the guidance, the direction, or what have you, of anybody connected with the American government? *Abrams:* Absolutely. That	"*Q:* I take it there came a time when a plane was shot down in Nicaragua and a Mr. Hasenfus parachuted down to safety and there were press accounts of it?...But, it would be quite untrue, would it not, to say that there was no connection with the NSC? *Poindexter:* There was...obviously

would be illegal....
Novak: Now, when you say you give categorical assurance, we're not playing word games that are so common in Washington. You're not talking about the NSC, or something else?
Abrams: I am not playing games.
Novak: National Security Council?
Abrams: No government agencies, none. "

Elliot Abrams,
Assistant Secretary of State for
Inter-American Affairs,
Interviewed on CNN's Evans and
Novak program,
October 11, 1986

knowledge by the NSC as to what the private organization was doing. There was coordination.
Q: Well, this was [retired Air Force Major General Richard] Secord's organization?
Poindexter: That's correct...Col North clearly understood what was happening and there was close cooperation between Col North and Gen. Secord. "

John Poindexter,
former National Security Advisor,
before the Joint Select Committee,
July 17, 1987

"We didn't have anything to do with the guy. We didn't have anything to do with the plane. And we can say that instead of our usual 'No comment,' because a plane that flies in and drops supplies would violate congressional restrictions. We have not and will not violate congressional restrictions."

Kathy Pherson,
CIA Spokesperson,
October 10, 1986

'*Mike Wallace:* What's an American sitting at home to make of all this?
Eugene Hasenfus: He's gonna make that our government is backing this one hundred percent, and that's what I believe, too.
Mike Wallace: So, in effect, what you're saying is that you felt, in the final analysis, that you were working for the -- for the U.S. government?
Eugene Hasenfus: Yes, sir.
Mike Wallace: For the CIA?
Eugene Hasenfus: Yes, sir. "

Eugene Hasenfus,
Interviewed on CBS's 60 Minutes News
Program,
October 19, 1986

"[Hasenfus] said that from 24 to 26 'company people' [CIA personnel] assisted the program in El Salvador, including flight crews, maintenance crews and two Cuban nationalized Americans that worked for the CIA."

Christian Science Monitor
October 10, 1986

"...I would like to state categorically that the crew of the C-123 aircraft which crashed on 5 October in Nicaragua were not CIA employees, nor do they work for us in any way. "

Clair George,
Deputy Director for Operations,
CIA,
before the House Select Committee on Intelligence,
October 14, 1986

"The [preceding October 14] statement, reading it legally and tightly, and I will apologize, I would like to apologize. You could say I was wrong....But technically, I apologize. I'm wrong."

Clair George,
before the Joint Select Committee,
August 6, 1987

X. THE CIA ROLE

ISSUE: Did the CIA play a role in the contra resupply operation in violation of legal restrictions forbidding such assistance?

ADMINISTRATION POSITION	COUNTEREVIDENCE
"...what you've got to understand is we were barred from being involved with the contras, and we kept away from that." *William Casey,* *Director of the CIA,* *Interview with Time Magazine,* *December 22, 1986*	"*Q.* [Were there] any other people [in the CIA] aware of your full-service operation [to aid the contras]? *A.* There was ample indication frequently that there was resupply going on from 1984 through 1986... Director Casey had specific and detailed knowledge because I briefed him frequently and in detail." *Oliver North,* *NSC Director of Political-Military Affairs,* *before the Joint Select Committee,* *July 8, 1987*

Casey

"I believe I was receiving support from the director of central intelligence [Casey]...we received some support from a senior CIA officer in Honduras."

Richard Secord,
Retired Air Force Major General who supervised contra resupply operations,
before the Joint Select Committee,
May 5, 1987,

"Director Casey testified under oath before four congressional committees that he did not learn that monies may have been diverted to the contras until the White House so informed him just before Attorney General Edwin Meese held his press conference on 25 November." *Statement by Sharon Foster,* *CIA Office of Public Affairs,* *January 9, 1987*	"Director Casey learned about [diverting profits from Iran arms sales to the contras] before the fact. [He] used several words to describe how he felt about it, all of which were effusive. He referred to it as 'the ultimate irony, the ultimate covert operation.'" *Oliver North,* *before the Joint Select Committee* *July 8, 1987* "'You [Casey] knew, didn't you', I said. 'The contra diversion had to be the first question. You knew all along.' His head jerked up hard. He stared, and finally nodded yes." *Bob Woodward,* *Veil: The Underground Wars of* *the CIA, 1981-1987* *Simon & Schuster, 1987*
"The CIA is not involved directly or indirectly in arranging, directing or facilitating resupply missions conducted by private individuals in support of the Nicaraguan Democratic Resistance." *Clair George,* *Deputy Director of Operations,* *CIA,* *before the House Select* *Committee on Intelligence,* *October 14, 1986*	"My participation did facilitate the private network because it provided information that permitted the supply drops to rebels inside Nicaragua to take place." *Joe Fernandez [aka Tomas Castillo],* *CIA Station Chief in Costa Rica,* *Disagreeing with George's October 14* *statement,* *before the Joint Select Committee,* *May 29, 1987*

"All I can say is that the CIA has complied with all congressional restrictions on assistance to the contras." *Kathy Pherson,* *CIA Spokesperson* *January 17, 1987*	"With the $27 million in Nicaraguan humanitarian assistance and the $3 million in communications equipment, training assistance, we were able to provide the Southern Front commanders with some measure of communications equipment and communications security, equipment and training." *Joe Fernandez [aka Tomas Castillo],* *CIA Station Chief in Costa Rica,* *before the Joint Select Committee,* *May 29, 1987*
	"In view of possible difficulties in obtaining supplemental appropriations to carry out the Nicaraguan covert action project through the remainder of this year, I am in full agreement that you should explore funding alternatives with the [deleted] others. I believe your thought of putting one of your staff in touch with the appropriate [deleted] official should promptly be pursued." *William J. Casey,* *Letter to Robert McFarlane, National* *Security Advisor,* *March 27, 1984*

"Intelligence will not be provided [to the contras] for the purposes of enabling or assisting the Nicaraguan opposition to conduct offensive military or paramilitary operations." *William J. Casey,* *Letter to David Durenburger* *Chairman, Senate Select* *Committee on Intelligence,* *March 18, 1985*	"*Q:* What was your understanding of the law...on the subject of Central Intelligence Agency passing intelligence to the contras? *A:* It was my understanding that intelligence could not be passed to the contras, period. *Q:* Were you aware at the time that Oliver North was seeking to...pass...intelligence to the contras [about the Sandinista's helicopters]? *A:* I don't remember the details of those discussions in passing information to him, but I undoubtedly did do that." *Alan Fiers,* *Director of CIA's Central American Task Force,* *before the Joint Select Committee,* *August 5, 1987*
"The CIA is asked to report on events in Central America, and among things they report on to us is some of this activity. But they do not direct it, directly or indirectly, wink or nod, or steer people. It's illegal. " *Elliot Abrams,* *Assistant Secretary of State for* *Inter-American Affairs,* *in Washington Post,* *November 9, 1986*	"*Fiers:* ...Elliot [Abrams] said I'm off to Brunei, I have a possibility of soliciting some money...he said how do we handle it? I said the best way to handle it is to go to [name of contra official deleted] and have him open a bank account... *Q:* Who was going to control the money? *Fiers:* [name of contra official deleted]... *Q:* Would he be overseen in doing that by the United States? *Fiers:* Absolutely." *Alan Fiers,* *Director of CIA Central American Task Force,* *before the Joint Select Committee,* *August 5, 1987*

"*Meese:* Bank accounts were established as best we know by representatives of the forces in Central America.
Q: Is there any evidence to indicate that those bank accounts were set up by the CIA?
Meese: No, there's no indication at all.
Q: With the help of the CIA?
Meese: No there's no indication whatsoever. To the best of our knowledge, no one in the CIA knew anything about it."

Edwin Meese,
Attorney General
November 25, 1986

"*Q:* Now you also received an account number subsequently from the chief of the Agency's Central American Task Force, correct?
Abrams: Correct.
Q:.....Now you had two account numbers [other account obtained from North]. How did you decide which account number to use for the actual solicitation [of funds for the contras from Brunei]?
Abrams: [We] did not really want to...be in a situation where the CIA would be in charge of this account ...and we weren't keen on...that idea of enhancing the role of the CIA...we thought that the account number which we were getting from Colonel North would be cleaner."

Elliot Abrams,
before the Joint Select Committee,
June 2, 1987

Meese

XI. OBSTRUCTION OF JUSTICE

ISSUE: Were Justice Department officials, including Attorney General Edwin Meese, knowledgeable about the illegal gunrunning operations to the contras prior to Meese's public disclosure of the scandal in November, 1986? If so, did these officials attempt to obstruct investigations into these operations taking place in Miami in 1985-1986?

ADMINISTRATION POSITION	COUNTEREVIDENCE
"In addition you should be aware that there have been allegations in the media that the Justice Department has ignored pro-contra criminal activity and that you and former Deputy Attorney General Jensen specifically instructed United States Attorney Leon Kellner in Miami to slow down or kill an investigation into alleged pro-contra gunrunning. Our inquiry has shown these last allegations to be totally baseless." *William F. Weld, Assistant Attorney General, Memo to Edwin Meese, Attorney General, November 14, 1986*	"Please get on top of this. D.L.J. [D. Lowell Jensen, former Deputy Attorney General] is giving a heads up to the NSC [National Security Council]. He would like us to watch over it. Call Leon [Kellner], find out what is up and advise him that decisions should be run by you." *Stephen Trott, Associate Attorney General, to Mark Richard, Deputy Assistant Attorney General in the Criminal Division, Handwritten note attached to secret Justice Department memo concerning contra gunrunning investigation, March 24, 1986*
	"Spoke to Kellner...file - contra folder." *Mark Richard, Deputy Assistant Attorney General, Handwritten note indicating he carried out Trott's instructions, attached to file memo about contra gunrunning, March 26, 1986*

ADMINISTRATION POSITION	COUNTEREVIDENCE
"*Q:* Can you tell us specifically if you spoke to anyone else at the NSC besides Admiral Poindexter or at the White House, about the Miami investigation? *Meese:* I have no recollection of this coming up in any conversation." *Edwin Meese,* *newsconference statement,* *April 6, 1987*	"*Dutton:* [T]he FAA [Federal Aviation Administration] and Customs [Bureau officials] arrived at Southern Air Transport and had said that they would like to look at the records...for Southern Air Transport [the company for which Dutton worked that helped coordinate the contra resupply operations]... *Q:* What did you do? *Dutton:* I called Col. North and he said [to] call him back. I called Col North [back] and he said he had spoken to Mr. Meese and that it would be taken care of." *Robert Dutton,* *retired Air Force colonel employed by Southern Air Transport who supervised contra resupply operations,* *before the Joint Select Committee,* *May 2, 1987*
"I can give you a categorical, on the record denial that the attorney-general or anyone else from Washington has applied pressure on me [to slow down investigation of contra resupply operations based in Florida]." *Leon Kellner,* *US Attorney in Miami,* *The Village Voice,* *December 30, 1986*	"[Assistant US Attorney David Leiwant] was called into Kellner's office and asked some advice on Neutrality Act violations, munitions exportations...and the Boland Amendment... In the office was Jeff Feldman. Feldman had just come back from Costa Rica and had interviewed the same witnesses I had...Jeff Feldman says,'God, I've got to tell you I've uncovered incredible things in Costa Rica, corroborating what a lot of people have alleged. Kellner looked at him and said, 'Don't you understand what I've been telling you? We're under a

great deal of pressure from Washington...I'm telling you, go very, very slow...Washington told me to take it slow.'
I can now say that Leon Kellner was obstructing justice. He was taking a criminal investigation and slowing it down for political reasons.
And my friend [Assistant US Attorney David Leiwant], who works for Kellner almost directly, says Kellner is in touch almost on a daily basis with Edwin Meese, and his underlings Trott and Jensen, and has been for almost eight months now."

John Mattes,
Attorney with the Federal Public Defender's Office in Miami, who first uncovered the Miami-based gunrunning operations,
Public statement,
August 23, 1986

"...in accordance with a request from Associate Attorney General Steve Trott, the Bureau [FBI] was to suspend its ongoing investigation of the captioned matter [Southern Air Transport's role in the contra resupply operations]...
As you know, this matter involves Eugene Hasenfus, the crew member of the C123 aircraft shot down over Nicaragua...The Bureau is anxious to resume its investiga-

	tion, but, even though the 10-day period requested by Steve Trott has expired, it is unwilling to do so without the [Justice] Department's approval."
	John L. Martin,
	Justice Department Criminal Division,
	memo to William Weld, Assistant
	Attorney General,
	November 12, 1986

ISSUE: Several Congressmen have faulted Meese for not treating his fact-finding inquiries between November 21 - 25 as a criminal investigation, given the evidence that Meese and his aides had knowledge of the criminal connections with the contra resupply operations. Was Meese's mishandling of the inquiry a deliberate attempt to obstruct justice by allowing principal figures in the scandal to destroy incriminating evidence?

ADMINISTRATION POSITION	COUNTEREVIDENCE
"I'd have to say that everyone [in the Justice Dept] has performed in an appropriate manner...The Attorney General has, at every step of the way, performed professionally and ethically."	"In a private deposition to the committees, North's deputy, Marine Lt. Col. Robert L. Earl, said North told him on Nov. 21 that he had just talked with the attorney general and learned that he had '24 or 48 hours' [to prepare for Meese's investigation], according to Rep. Peter W. Rodino...who said he had seen a transcript of Earl's sworn testimony."
Terry Eastland,	
Justice Department Spokesman,	*Washington Post,*
in New York Times,	*July 28, 1987*
December 14, 1986	

ADMINISTRATION POSITION	COUNTEREVIDENCE

"I had no information from Secretary [of State] Shultz at all about any concern or knowledge that he had of any overlap between the Iranian initiative and the contra funding. That was not in any way discussed...at the meeting that I had with... Shultz that morning [November 22]"

Edwin Meese,
before the Joint Select
Committee,
July 28, 1987

Shultz

"*Q:* The notes of your interview with the Attorney General reflect, among other things, your expressing the concern to him on that Saturday that this Iran matter, or fear that this Iran matter would somehow get wrapped into aid to the Nicaraguan resistance. What was the basis for that fear that you expressed on Saturday the 22nd? *Shultz:* Because somebody had pointed out to me that the --I think it is the Southern Air Transport was used in the Central American situation, and also in terms of the flights of arms [to Iran] and so I said, quote, 'Well my gosh, if this gets connected, then we are going to have a problem with our policy in Central America.'"

George Shultz,
Secretary of State,
before the Joint Select Committee,
July 24, 1987

"*Q:* Mr. Attorney General, you...were aware of the Judiciary Committee independent counsel request... regarding the Hasenfus flight ...And that request specifically named the Vice President, [CIA]Director Casey, [Defense] Secretary Weinberger, [National Security Advisor] Admiral Poindexter and Oliver North as individuals to be investigated. All these individuals were on your list to be interviewed during your fact-finding inquiry as well. Didn't [this]...raise concerns in your mind...about the propriety of speaking to these individuals without criminal investigators present? *Meese:* It never raised any at all..."

Edwin Meese,
before the Joint Select
Committee,
July 28, 1987

"*Weld:* My exact words, as best I can recall, were I am not sure it makes very much sense for the Criminal Division and the FBI not to be involved in this [Meese's November fact-finding].
Q: ...Did you also make any comments regarding the Attorney General being used as a fact-gatherer?
Weld: ...I could not see the wisdom of that.*"

William Weld,
Assistant Attorney General, Criminal Division,
in deposition before the Joint Select Committee,
July 16, 1987

"So there was at no time any attempt to keep the criminal division out of anything that had criminal implications"

Edwin Meese,
before the Joint Select
Committee,
July 28, 1987

"*Q:*...And when he [Meese] called you, what did he say to you?
Weld:...He said words to the effect of, "I just want you to know that with respect to this Iran matter that the fact that the Criminal Division is not involved is not negligence or sloppiness...This is being done that way on purpose".

William Weld,
in deposition before the Joint Select
Committee,
July 16, 1987

Part 2:
The Reagan Record on Central America: The First Term 1981-1984

P R E F A C E

In 1973, Senator Sam Ervin, in charge of the Select committee investigating possible criminal implications of the Watergate affair, held an exchange with Commerce Secretary Maurice Stans, who was also finance chairman of the Committee to Re-Elect the President. Senator Ervin inquired about why Stans had destroyed certain records of funds. Stans said that there was nothing illegal about it. Ervin said that the law didn't require Stans to destroy records, did it? Stans replied that "the law didn't even require us to keep records in the first place."

"Do you think," Ervin asked, "that men of great influence and power like yourself and the Attorney General of the United States should content themselves with merely staying on the windy side of the law?"

As it turned out the individuals of great power had gone beyond "the windy side" of the law and had broken the letter of the law itself. Watergate is remembered for the violations of law by the most powerful political figures of the nation; not only for the break-in at Democratic Party headquarters, but for the illegal bombing of Cambodia, the CIA involvements in assassinations and coups, all of which came into public view in the 1973-75 period. It was a period of shame that is still associated in the public mind with the very mention of the words Vietnam and Watergate.

Logical and direct links existed between the Nixon White House's obsession with "leaks" about bombing and invasion plans in Southeast Asia, and the creation of the "plumbers" to find those leaks and repair them.

The break-ins at former Administration official Daniel Ellsberg's psychiatrist's office and the Watergate offices of the Democratic Party, Nixon's attempts to manipulate the

CIA, using "national security" as the pretext, all derive from attempts, begun long before Nixon, to manipulate Congress, to go beyond the constitutional limits of the executive, to attempt, as Senator Ervin put it, to stay not within the spirit and letter of the law, but to feel that it is sufficient just to stay on the "windy side."

As with the experience in Southeast Asia, so too with the present Central American policy, an Administration is so obsessed with pursuing its policy goals that it has been unwilling to learn the lessons of the Watergate-Vietnam-CIA scandal period. The law, once again, has become less important than policy goals, as if a ruling has been handed down that God has mandated a policy, and that His intervention automatically takes precedence over the US Constitution. If God is indeed speaking to the small group inside the Administration that makes Central America policy, He has not seen fit to speak to Congress, the press, nor indeed, to the majority of US citizens who have indicated their opposition to the policy lines.

We witnessed just over a decade ago how our political system could suffer from debilitating and demoralizing scandals caused by abuses of the law, and by a President who cared little for the spirit of the law. We see today in the Administration's attempts to circumvent Congressional restrictions on Central American aid; on its sneaking of funds appropriated for one purpose in Honduras into a non-authorized military project; on the shady use of American military personnel in El Salvador and possibly Nicaragua; on the constant fudging, withholding, distorting and downright lying about the facts in Central America, all the ingredients that were present at the time when this nation was humiliated by the activities of its most powerful leaders. The ingredients of scandal, however, may be even less serious than the formula for stripping away Congress' fragile hold on the war-making power, by simply refusing to acknowledge its authority. That step can lead not only to new and deadly interventionist adventures, but to the de facto alteration of our political system.

Conservatives, which the leading Administration officials and its backers call themselves, have learned from history, and stood firmly on the side of law and order to preserve the virtuous essences of the past, the institutions, values and ways of behaving. Real conservatives have heeded the advice of Edmund Burke who counseled that "A Conservative man would be cautious how he dealt in blood." Some of today's alleged conservatives have literally thrown away the historical record, have spat upon the law of the land and can hardly wait to spill blood. Their excuse of course is that a demonic enemy which threatens us all forces us to abandon the dictates of our conservative ancestors and throw caution to the wind.

UN Ambassador Kirkpatrick declared in 1981 that the Soviet-Cuban menace makes Central America "the most important place in the world for the United States today." The President has reiterated that statement. More prudent however, may be the analysis of US Ambassador to Panama Ambler Moss who stated in 1980, "What we see in Central America today would not be much different if Fidel Castro and the Soviet Union did not exist." Mr. Moss has read history, which began long before Fidel Castro was born, and indeed, even preceded the Bolshevik revolution.

If we are to persevere as a republic, we must place regard for our own institutions at the very top of our priority list and pay close attention to the real conservatives in American life and history. One of them, President John Quincy Adams, offered words of wisdom to all those who would claim the conservative heritage:

> "The true American goes not abroad in search of monsters to destroy. . . . (America) well knows that by once enlisting under other banners than her own, were they even the banners of foreign independence, she would involve herself, beyond the power of extrication, in all wars of interest and intrigue, of individual avarice, envy, and ambition. She might become the dictatress of the world: she would no longer be the ruler of her own spirit."

> July 4, 1821
> John Quincy Adams

The Honorable George McGovern

INTRODUCTION

The well-being of the American system of government depends upon a stable system of checks and balances between the executive and legislative branches. The executive relies on the appropriations and political support of Congress to execute its policies. The legislature, in turn, must count on the cooperation of the Executive to keep it fully informed and abide by its legislative authority. This interdependence is as pivotal to our notion of representative democracy as it is fragile. As U.S. intervention in Vietnam demonstrated, both the trust that is fundamental to our democracy and the constitutional balance between the branches can be major casualties of war.

Unfortunately, escalating U.S. involvement in Central America has spawned a credibility gap that threatens the constitutional order once again. Whether testifying on the state of human rights in El Salvador and Guatemala, the scope of CIA activities targeted against the government of Nicaragua, or the scale of the growing U.S. military buildup in Honduras, Reagan Administration officials have misled Congress about the nature of its activities and goals in Central America. The disturbingly systematic record of such deceit has prompted this report.

The contrast is stark between claims made by Reagan officials before Congress and the reality of U.S. policy we are documenting here. From this juxtaposition, it appears that the Administration has violated the law in a number of instances. In other cases, the disparity between Administration proclamations and the gathered evidence indicates that while the White House has not violated a law, it has at least been contemptuous of the spirit of the law and/or the intent of Congress.

The introductions to each of the following chapters serve to outline how Administration deception is pertinent to possible violations of congressional acts, Executive orders, domestic laws and international agreements. The intent of these laws is summarized, and the relevant passages are cited, in the appendix of this report. Each issue involving Administration deceit before Congress is arranged under broad categories for each country. For example, in the chapter on El Salvador, issues fall under the subheadings of Progress on Government Reforms, Human Rights, Hostilities Endangering U.S. Personnel, and Appropriations. The substantive arguments surrounding each issue are then summarized in a brief paragraph. Under this issue description, the Executive Branch's position as stated during congressional testimony by an Administration official is quoted directly. This testimony, by one or more Administration officials, is then contrasted against internal government cables and documents, congressional studies, reports by respected nongovernmental organizations, and press accounts.

Reagan Administration distortions on Central America break down into the following types of statements:

- Statements about what the executive branch is actually doing. This includes, for example, denials about the mining of Nicaragua's harbors, which subsequent revelations demonstrated to be lies.

- Statements on a situation about which the Administration withholds information, or knows the circumstances to be otherwise. Such was the case, for example, in the charges that Nicaragua supplied most of the Salvadoran rebel arms in early 1983, despite a cable from the U.S. embassy in San Salvador which reported that the rebels were supplied by capturing most of their weapons from the Salvadoran Army.

- Statements about the Administration's overall goals for each country and for the region. Officials, for example, repeatedly said that they are not seeking to overthrow the Government of Nicaragua or establish a permanent military presence in Honduras. Counter-evidence gathered here suggests just the opposite intentions.

WHY DECEPTION?

The weighty accumulation of deception practiced by the Reagan Administration underscores a fundamental reality of United States policy towards Central America: the nature of the regimes and movements bolstered by U.S. assistance, and the Administration's ultimate policy goals for the entire region, are repugnant to basic U.S. values. It is only through deception that the American people may be beguiled into accepting the current policy, and the Congress may be manipulated into legitimating escalating intervention. Consider each of the countries in turn:

NICARAGUA: Each successive year, the Reagan Administration has expanded its agenda of military and para-military activities against the Government of Nicaragua. In November 1981, CIA Director William Casey secured $19 million from Congress for a "minimal" secret operation with the stated purpose of "interdicting" arms allegedly flowing from Nicaragua to the Salvadoran rebels. As the original "contra" force of 500 to 1,000 Nicaraguan exiles swelled to the present army of 10-15,000 soldiers—trained, equipped and directed by the CIA—their purpose also expanded, as did their range of activities against the Sandinista government. Public disclosures of the CIA's contra manual and its mining of Nicaragua's harbors exploded the interdiction rationale and exposed the true intent of the CIA's contra war: to destabilize the Nicaraguan government.

In February 1985, while campaigning to restore funds to the contras suspended in late 1984, President Reagan brazenly admitted to wanting to "remove" the Sandinista government—or making it cry "uncle." The Administration's candor—finally unveiling its long-concealed objectives—appeared to openly violate international agreements in the O.A.S. and U.N. charters, and the Boland Amendment, a law passed by Congress prohibiting U.S. efforts at toppling the Nicaraguan government.

During its efforts to renew further funding for the covert war, the Administration claimed that money for the contras was running out. However, the contras have maintained a consistent level of logistical activities. Several published reports and Administration documents suggest that the White House is carrying out an "end run" around Congress by finding alternative sources of funding for its undeclared war against Managua.

EL SALVADOR: During its first term in office, the Reagan Administration increased U.S. involvement in the war in El Salvador from a $25 million outlay in military assistance in March 1981 to $196 million in military aid in fiscal year 1984. U.S. military and economic assistance to El Salvador during those four years totalled over $1 billion. Moreover, U.S. personnel have trained thousands of Salvadoran troops, have flown reconnaissance missions over combat zones, and have gained influence—if not control—over the direction of the war itself.

The size and intensity of the war has escalated alongside the U.S commitment. The Salvadoran military—which numbered 12,000 men in 1981—stands at 45,000 today. The guerilla army has kept pace, tripling from 4,000 fighters in 1981 to its present force of 12,000. The FDR/FMLN controls an estimated 20-25% of the nation's territory. Forty-five thousand Salvadorans have been killed over the past five years. The Salvadoran human rights monitors, *Socorro Juridico* and *Tutela Legal*, attribute at least 80% of the killings to government military, security and para-military forces.

Between mid-1981 and mid-1983, Congress conditioned U.S. military aid to El Salvador on the certification by the Reagan Administration that reforms on human rights and land tenure had been achieved. In these certification hearings and in other testimony, Administration officials misrepresented the status of such reforms—as well as the security situation of U.S. personnel in the country.

HONDURAS: Since the beginning of 1983, Honduras has played an integral role in the Reagan Administration's regional policy in Central

America. For the last two years, the United States has staged almost continuous joint exercises with Honduras, which have brought up to 5,000 U.S. servicemen to the Central American nation. The Administration has also conducted simultaneous naval maneuvers off both coasts of Central America which involved as many as 30,000 U.S. troops.

The Administration's slow but steady militarization of Honduras—a buildup admittedly aimed at the Sandinistas and the Salvadoran rebels—has been constructed virtually behind the backs of Congress and the public. Under the guise of routine military maneuvers, the Administration has erected an infrastructure for intervention—improving or building airfields, base camps, radar facilities, fuel depots and a major training center. During hearings on Capitol Hill, White House officials performed linguistic somersaults in order to elude Congressional queries concerning the extent and implications of the expanding U.S. presence.

GUATEMALA: Although the amount of U.S. assistance to Guatemala pales in comparison with that provided to El Salvador, the Reagan Administration has quietly increased material aid in support of the Guatemalan government's counter-insurgency programs. The White House is seeking to boost military assistance from $300,000 in the current fiscal year to $35.3 million for next year.

Before and since the Reagan Administration took office, the Guatemalan government and military have repressed all forms of popular organization and expression—ranging from guerilla movements and peasant organizations to trade unions, churches, teacher's groups and the media. Repression has been particularly targeted against the country's indigenous population living in the rural areas of the countryside. Since 1981, the White House has chipped away at the embargo imposed by the Carter Administration, which denied direct U.S. military assistance to the Guatemalan regime because of its gross violations of human rights.

Over the past four years, the Administration's actions with respect to Guatemala have included:

- Licensing the sale of military jeeps and trucks.
- Authorizing the sale of spare parts for "Huey" combat helicopters.
- Sending $300,000 in military assistance.
- Voting for tens of millions of dollars in international loans by multilateral lending institutions.

These measures have been taken in the face of human rights reports by groups such as Amnesty International, which have documented widespread abuses against civilians under the regimes of Generals Lucas Garcia, Rios Montt and Mejia Victores. A number of these actions—particularly those including military assistance—appear to directly violate U.S. laws which prohibit military sales, multilateral loans and security assistance to countries which are gross and consistent violators of human rights. Reagan officials have circumvented such laws by either disputing the potential military application of the sales they have approved, or by denying the severity of human rights abuses inside Guatemala.

THE PRICE OF DECEIT

A consideration of the current U.S. policy towards Central America—the expanded covert war against Nicaragua, unending military assistance to El Salvador, the U.S. military buildup in Honduras, renewed military aid to Guatemala—leads to the question of whether the Reagan Administration is seeking military or diplomatic solutions in the region. The matter of deceit is central to this question. The most promising avenue for reaching a peaceful settlement in the region has been through the Contadora group of nations—Columbia, Panama, Mexico and Venezuela—who have been working to develop a formula for a satisfactory peace accord. Reagan officials repeatedly told Congress of the high regard they have for the Contadora process. However, late last year, a briefing paper prepared for a meeting of the National Security Council was obtained by the press. The document boasted that the Administration "effectively blocked Contadora group efforts" to reach an agreement on a revised draft peace treaty. Although Reagan officials later complained that the treaty lacked adequate verification measures, critics reasonably can question how serious the Administration is about reaching a diplomatic solution to the region's conflicts.

When promises of peace and negotiated settlements serve as mere window dressing for secret wars, murder manuals and escalating militarization, Congress and the public are robbed of their voice to debate and influence the conduct of foreign affairs. Herein lies the deadly connection between deception and democracy. Democracy demands public debate and informed consent. Neither is possible when the President misleads legislators and voters as to the nature of its allies, actions and agendas in distant and nearby lands. When such is the case—as in Central America today—contempt of Congress also becomes contempt for the American people.

NICARAGUA

The Reagan Administration's war against Nicaragua has become the centerpiece of its Central America policy. The Administration's cavalier attitude towards legal restrictions which should govern its actions toward Nicaragua exemplifies its approach to the law with respect to all of Central America. There are seven prominent laws, treaties, and other formal prohibitions that the Administration appears to have violated, or has been contemptuous of in spirit, in its dealings with Nicaragua. These restrictions can be grouped into six categories, with some laws falling into more than one category: the purpose of the covert war, CIA spending limits, mining Nicaragua's harbors, political assassination and terrorism, Nicaragua's military build-up, and the War Powers Act.

I. THE PURPOSE OF THE COVERT WAR

The President signed into law on December 21, 1982 the *Boland Amendment*, which prohibited the use of funds for the purpose of overthrowing the Government of Nicaragua. The public record suggests that the Administration violated the amendment on several occasions. In December 1984, a majority of the House Intelligence Committee found that a CIA manual advocating the "overthrow" of the Nicaraguan Government represented a violation of the Boland Amendment.

In addition, internal Administration documents along with the CIA Contra Comic Book and statements by contra leaders dramatize the Administration contempt for the Boland Amendment.

Subsequent acts of Congress reaffirmed the intent of the Boland Amendment. However, in a nationally televised press conference on February 21, 1985 President Reagan stated explicitly that the Administration policy was to have the Sandinista government "removed in the sense of its present structure" unless the present government was willing to say "uncle".

II. CIA SPENDING LIMITS

In funding the covert war, the Reagan Administration may have violated a number of legal restrictions. When Congress enacted the *Defense Appropriations Act of 1984* on December 8 1983, it limited to $24 million the amount of funds which could be expended "directly or indirectly" for support of military or paramilitary operations against Nicaragua. Evidence, however, suggests that the Reagan Administration circumvented this funding cap. The House Committee on Intelligence identified several possible departures from the CIA's own guidelines for complying with the FY 84 spending "cap" and has begun further investigation.

Congress signed a Continuing Resolution on October 12, 1984 which suspended all funds that directly or indirectly supported the contra forces in Nicaragua. The resolution stipulated that funding could be renewed only upon approval by both houses of Congress after February 28, 1985. The Reagan Administration may have attempted to circumvent this congressional ban by soliciting the aid of third countries in supporting its covert activities and using the resources of the Department of Defense.

III. THE MINING OF NICARAGUA'S HARBORS

Under the *Intelligence Oversight Act of 1980*, the CIA is legally obligated to provide full and current reports of its activities to Congress. The Oversight Act serves to restrict the scope and power of the CIA, prohibiting it from acting autonomously in foreign affairs. Nevertheless, the CIA has failed to properly inform congressional oversight committees concerning its activities in Nicaragua. For instance, between February and April 1984, mines exploding in Nicaraguan harbors damaged a dozen merchant freighters from 6 countries. Six weeks after the initial detonation, CIA officials finally offered detailed testimony to the Senate Intelligence Committee concerning the degree of U.S. involvement in the mining operation.

IV. POLITICAL ASSASSINATION AND SUPPORT FOR TERRORISM

Increased reports that CIA-backed rebels engaged in terrorist activities have brought into question both the integrity and the legality of CIA involvement in Nicaragua. In September 1984, Congress received a document entitled "Psychological Operations in Guerrilla Warfare." The manual offers explicit instruction in "neutralizing" Sandinista officials and "creating martyrs" for the contra cause. President Reagan, in response to the public uproar generated by the primer, called it "much ado about nothing" even though the manual appears to constitute a violation of the President's own *Executive Order 12333* which prohibits the involvement of any U.S. agency in assassinations.

V. THE ALLEGED ARMS BUILDUP

In an effort to justify its intervention in Nicaragua, the Reagan Administration has repeatedly invoked the "collective self-defense" clause of the UN and OAS Charters. The U.S. claims that Nicaragua's purported military build-up is a prelude to future aggression and that the U.S. has an obligation to defend Nicaragua's neighbors. However, the public record suggests that the Administration is not acting in collective self-defense but rather is inflating the extent and nature of Nicaragua's military arsenal and exaggerating the degree of Soviet and Cuban involvement in Nicaragua.

VI. THE WAR POWERS ACT

According to the stipulations of the *War Powers Act*, the Reagan Administration is required, in the absence of a declaration of war, to fully inform Congress when U.S. forces are introduced into potentially hostile areas. Public reports indicate numerous instances in which U.S. forces encountered hostilities in the vicinity of Nicaragua. In none of these cases did the Administration notify Congress.

I. THE PURPOSE OF THE "COVERT" WAR

ISSUE: For the first three years of the covert operation against Nicaragua, the Administration denied that it intended to overthrow the Nicaraguan government. In late February 1985, President Reagan admitted his objective of removing the "present structure" of the Sandinista government. Did the Administration conceal its objective of overthrowing the Nicaraguan government?

ADMINISTRATION POSITION	COUNTEREVIDENCE
"The United States does not seek to destabilize or overthrow the Government of Nicaragua nor to impose or compel any particular form of government there." *Letter from President Reagan to Senate Majority Leader Howard Baker April 4, 1984*	". . . a commandante of ours will literally be able to shake up the Sandinista structure, and replace it. . . . This is the moment in which the overthrow can be achieved and our revolution can become an open one . . ." *from "Psychological Operations and Guerilla Warfare" Manual produced by the CIA for Nicaraguan Contras Fall, 1983*
"But let us be clear as to the American attitude toward the Government of Nicaragua. We do not seek its overthrow." *President Reagan before Joint Session of Congress April 27, 1983*	"I remember he [a CIA official] said he was speaking on behalf of the president of the United States who was very interested in getting rid of the Sandinistas." *Edgar Chamorro, former FDN Directorate member, recalling incident in late 1982. Washington Post November 27, 1984*
 *Reagan*	"Three years ago, as the administration assured Congress that ousting Nicaragua's leftist government was not a U.S. goal, CIA paramilitary officers prepared an ambitious plan to achieve that objective, according to U.S. officials. One knowledgeable official . . . said a timetable for overthrowing the Sandinista regime by the end of 1983 was written by senior CIA paramilitary officers in early 1982 . . ." *Washington Post February 24, 1985*
"We have made clear repeatedly that the Administration is not trying to overthrow the Nicaraguan government . . ." *Langhorne A. Motley, Assistant Secretary of State for Inter-American Affairs. Written response*	"participate in the final battle . . ." *"Freedom Fighters Manual", Comic Book produced by the CIA for Nicaraguan contras Fall 1983* "This manual [CIA manual for Nicaraguan contras, Fall 1983] was written and printed up in several editions by

ADMINISTRATION POSITION	COUNTEREVIDENCE
to questions posed by the House Subcommittee on Western Hemisphere Affairs. *May 2, 1984*	the CIA. The manual talks of overthrowing the Sandinistas. . . . A majority of the Committee concludes that the manual represents a violation of the Boland Amendment." *House Select Committee on Intelligence,* *Press Release* *December 5, 1984*
"[W]e are not seeking to overthrow the Sandinista government." *Secretary of State George Shultz before the Senate Foreign Relations Committee,* *August 4, 1983*	DOD [the Department of Defense] believes that . . . either the resistance forces [the contras] fail . . . or they succeed, but that the President would be charged by Congress with violating the law regardless of outcome." *"Strategy for Central America," working paper prepared by an interagency task force for National Security Council Meeting* *July 6, 1983*
Q: "You're not doing anything to overthrow the government there [Nicaragua]?" A: "No, because that would be breaking the law." *President Reagan* *Press Conference* *April 17, 1983*	"It is my judgment that there has been an apparent violation of law. If you look at the stories that have come out of there, from reporters and members who have gone down there, the evidence is very strong." *Rep. Edward Boland, Chair of the House Intelligence Committee, New York Times* *April 14, 1983*

ISSUE: In congressional testimony, the Reagan Administration has justified its intervention in Nicaragua as an attempt to prevent Nicaragua from exporting arms to El Salvador. Has the Reagan Administration misrepresented the nature of Nicaragua's armed support for the Salvadoran guerillas?

ADMINISTRATION POSITION	COUNTEREVIDENCE
"The largest percentage of the munitions come in from Nicaragua, not through capturing U.S. supplies with government forces." *Fred Ikle, Undersecretary of Defense for Policy, before the Senate Subcommittee on Western Hemisphere Affairs,* *March 20, 1984*	"Since early 1983, it appears that the insurgents may have obtained most of their newly acquired firearms through capture from the Salvadoran military." *Cable from U.S. embassy in El Salvador to Washington,* *August 1983*

ADMINISTRATION POSITION	COUNTEREVIDENCE

"[T]he majority of the weapons still used by the [Salvadoran] guerrillas were supplied externally."

Langhorne Motley, before the House Subcommittee on Western Hemisphere Affairs February 21, 1984

Motley

"Since then (November 1980 to January 1981) except for special periods when new guerrilla units were being equipped or immediately before a major offensive, the flow has been sporadic. Ammunition, medicines, clothing—rather than weapons—often make up the bulk of the shipments."

"Nicaragua's Military Build-Up and Support for Central American Subversion," Joint publication of Department of Defense/Department of State Draft presented to members of Congress June 27, 1984

"There has not been a successful interdiction, or a verified report, of arms moving from Nicaragua to El Salvador since April 1981. . . . [T]he Administration and the CIA have systematically misrepresented Nicaraguan involvement in the supply of arms to Salvadoran guerrillas to justify efforts to overthrow the Nicaraguan Government."

David C. MacMichael, former CIA employee who provided national intelligence estimates on Central America from 1981 to 1983. Quoted in the New York Times June 11, 1984

". . .tons and tons of munitions are being flown in from Nicaragua."

Thomas Enders, Assistant Secretary of State for Inter-American Affairs before the House Subcommittee on Western Hemisphere Affairs March 1, 1983

Enders

"Intelligence officials claims they can 'hear a toilet flush in Managua,' yet they have not been able or free to produce a captured van, or downed air-airplane."

The Jacobsen Report, "Soviet Attitudes Towards, Aid to and Contacts With Central American Revolutionaries," Report Commissioned by the State Department's Bureau of Intelligence and Research June, 1984

II. CIA SPENDING LIMITS

ISSUE: Congress placed a $24 million funding cap on direct and indirect support of the anti-Sandinista rebels for fiscal year 1984. The CIA has testified that it has remained within the limit of the funding cap. Has the intelligence agency circumvented Congress and exceeded the cap in financing the covert war?

ADMINISTRATION POSITION	COUNTEREVIDENCE
"But a Republican on the Senate Intelligence Committee said [CIA] agency officials deny that they have spent more than the $24 million Congress approved for this fiscal year to fund 'contras' . . ." *Washington Post* *June 7, 1984*	"One [House Intelligence] committee member said this week that the intelligence agency charged some costs of the rebel program to accounts other than the ones covered by the $24 million . . . part of the cost of printing a rebel manual on guerrilla warfare was charged to the Office of Technical Services . . . the salaries of some agency employees sent to Honduras to work with the rebels was covered by normal payroll accounts. The agency also paid the living expenses for the families of several rebel leaders, but those costs were not charged to the $24 million account . . ." *New York Times* *January 13, 1985*
	"The Committee identified several possible departures from the CIA's own guidelines for complying with the FY 84 spending cap on aid to the contras." *House Committee on Intelligence, Press Release* *December 5, 1984*
"When asked about their accounting practices during committee hearings last year, intelligence agency officials said they had been using the same procedures for decades, intelligence committee members said." *New York Times* *January 13, 1985*	"[W]e believe that 1984 expenditures in assistance to the contras exceeded the $24 million ceiling . . . we strongly disagree with the accounting methods and principles used to track classified expenditures subject to the $24 million cap." *Letter to Caspar W. Weinberger, Secretary of Defense, from Rep. Joseph Addabbo and Rep. Norman Mineta* *January 30, 1985*

ISSUE: Did the Department of Defense circumvent the 1984 $24 million funding cap by providing its resources to the CIA and the anti-Sandinista rebels?

ADMINISTRATION POSITION	COUNTEREVIDENCE
"U.S. military exercise activities have no connection with anti-Sandinistas." *Pentagon response to question submitted by the House Committee on Appropriations March 1, 1984*  *Weinberger*	"Large amounts of equipment have been transferred from Defense to the CIA for the rebels according to Richard C. Lawrence, who until last fall was director of Central American affairs in the office of Nestor Sanchez assistance secretary for Inter-American affairs. "We gave the agency pretty much anything they wanted. . . . There is a terrible gray area about what to do in semi-declared wars." *Washington Post September 15, 1984* "The Defense Department, according to American officials and documents, has provided the CIA with ships, planes, guns and other equipment at nominal rates as well as free transport for use in the covert war in Nicaragua." *New York Times May 18, 1984*

ISSUE: Did the Defense Department ship "humanitarian" aid to those associated with the rebels although it was prohibited by law from such activity?

ADMINISTRATION POSITION	COUNTEREVIDENCE
"[W]e had the authority to do what we did. I continue to believe in the propriety of our actions in Honduras." *Defense Secretary Weinberger in response to accusations contained in June 22, 1984, report by the General Accounting Office New York Times July 1, 1984*	"The most concerted humanitarian effort was conducted during AHUS TARA [Big Pine] II. Between August 1983 and January 12, 1984, U.S. military personnel assigned to the exercise . . . transported over 1 million pounds of food for various private voluntary organizations. . . . The U.S Army's legal position on these activities, however, is that civic action and humanitarian projects cannot be conducted using O&M funds without a prior agreement on reimbursement. . . . We found no evidence of either reim-

bursement agreements or reimburse-
ments during our visit to Honduras."

*"GAO Responses To Questions In November 14,
1983, Letter," Report by the General Accounting
Office*

"[I]t is our conclusion that DOD's [De-
partment of Defense's] use of O&M
[Operating and Maintance] funds to finance civic/humanitarian activities during combined exercises in Honduras,
in the absence of an interagency order
or agreement under the Economy Act,
was an improper use of funds, in violation of 31 U.S.C. S 1301 (a)."

*Report by the General Accounting Office
June 22, 1984*

"With the approval of the Department
of Defense, the Pro-America Educa-
tional Foundation has used Fort
Meade, Maryland, and the Air National Guard Base at Selfridge, Michi-
gan to store supplies they collected this
spring for the contras. In May, the Air
Force flew the supplies from both
bases to Central America free of
charge."

*New York Times
July 15, 1984*

"One Congressional source said it was
understood that the Defense Department organized 10 to 15 missions to
carry the supplies [collected by private
groups] to Honduras in the last six
months. . . ."

*Miami Herald
September 9, 1984*

ISSUE: For fiscal year 1985, Congress suspended funding for activities which *directly or indirectly* supported military or para-military
operations in Nicaragua. Since the $24 million granted in fiscal
year 1984 was estimated to be expended in the spring of 1984,
no funds were provided to support the Nicaraguan insurgency
after June 1, 1984. Does the Reagan Administration continue to

indirectly support the covert war by soliciting other governments to fund the contras' activities?

ADMINISTRATION POSITION	COUNTEREVIDENCE
Mr. Gejdenson: ". . . Are you actively or is the administration actively trying to get other countries to play a major role in helping America with its efforts in Central America, either covert or overt? . . . Are we for instance trying to get the Israelis to play a more active role in helping with the Contras." . . . "Are there any specific countries that we have engaged to get additional military assistance?" *Mr. Motley*: "No." *Langhorne Motley, before the House Subcommittee on Western Hemisphere Affairs May 2, 1984*	"Action Plan: . . . The Secretary of State shall enlist the support of other countries (Israel, Venezuela, etc.) for military assistance and civic action projects." *"Strategy for Central America," working paper prepared by an interagency task force for National Security Council Meeting July 6, 1983*
"Representative Peter H. Kostmayer, a Pennsylvania Democrat, warned Mr. Motley that the use of back channels to avoid Congressional intent was a violation of law. Was this being done, the lawmaker asked the Administration official. 'The answer is no,' Mr. Motley said." *New York Times reporting January 29, 1985 testimony of Langhorne Motley before the House Western Hemisphere Subcommittee January 30, 1985*	"Israel . . . reportedly has secretly contributed $4-5 million to the rebels this year in response to a quietly made U.S. request." *Miami Herald September 9, 1984* "The White House is considering a bid to friendly Asian countries to help channel aid to the Nicaraguan rebels, a Reagan Administration official said today." *New York Times March 6, 1985*
"The [congressional] sources said the House and Senate intelligence oversight committees have since been pressing the CIA for a full accounting of the rebels' alternate sources of supply. So far, however, the CIA has declined to provide the	"Privately, however, administration sources said certain U.S. officials let it be known in the right places that the contras needed help because of congressional opposition to their cause and that the United States would make it up to these governments." *Miami Herald September 9, 1984*

ADMINISTRATION POSITION	COUNTEREVIDENCE
information maintaining that it now has little or no control over rebel activities." *Miami Herald* *September 9, 1984*	

III. THE MINING OF NICARAGUA'S HARBORS

ISSUE: The Intelligence Oversight Act requires the CIA to keep Congress fully and currently informed about intelligence activities. Was Congress properly informed about the mining of Nicaragua's principle seaports conducted in 1984? Was the U.S. mining of Nicaraguan ports a violation of international law?

ADMINISTRATION POSITION	COUNTEREVIDENCE
"I intend to comply fully with the spirit and the letter of the Intelligence Oversight Act. I intend to provide this committee with the information it believes it needs for oversight purposes." *William Casey, Director of the CIA, before the Senate Select Committee on Intelligence January 13, 1981*	". . . .the Committee [the Senate Select Committee] agreed that it was not adequately informed in a timely manner of certain significant intelligence activity in such a manner as to permit the Committee to carry out its oversight function. The Director of Central Intelligence concurred in that assessment." *Statement released by the Senate Select Committee on Intelligence, Approved by CIA Director Casey April 26, 1984.*
"We have fully met all statutory requirements for notifying our Intelligence Oversight Committees of the covert action program in Nicaragua. . . . [and] complied with the letter of the law in our briefings . . . [and] with the spirit as well." *Bulletin for CIA Employees, cited in the New York Times April 20, 1984*	"This appears to me to be the most emphatic way I can express my view that the Senate Committee was not properly briefed on the mining of Nicaraguan harbors with American mines from an American ship under American command. . . . In no event was the briefing 'full' 'current' or 'prior' as required by the Intelligence Oversight Act of 1980. . . ." *Senator Daniel Patrick Moynihan, In resignation of Vice Chair of the Senate Select Committee on Intelligence April 15, 1984*

ADMINISTRATION POSITION	COUNTEREVIDENCE
"... the United States is not mining the harbors of Nicaragua." *Caspar Weinberger, speaking on the ABC News program "This Week," April 8, 1984*	"... an inter-agency committee representing State, Defense and the CIA by the end of 1983 agreed on a package of measures including mining. The President approved the package...." *Newsweek April 23, 1984*
"Our purpose, in conformity with American and international law, is to prevent the flow of arms to El Salvador, Honduras, Guatemala and Costa Rica." *President Reagan, before Joint Session of Congress April 27, 1983*	"... the Court voted unanimously that the United States of America should immediately cease and refrain from any action restricting, blocking or endangering access to or from Nicaraguan ports, and in particular, the laying of mines." *International Court of Justice, The Hague May 10, 1984*
	"In adopting this amendment, the committee was particularly concerned with ensuring that U.S. assistance provided for interdiction activities in international territory not be used for actions, such as naval blockades, which are not permitted by international laws." *Boland–Zablocki Amendment December 9, 1983*

IV. POLITICAL ASSASSINATION AND SUPPORT OF TERRORISM

ISSUE: Is the Reagan Administration supporting and funding contra forces which are engaged in assassination in violation of the President's own Executive Order?

ADMINISTRATION POSITION	COUNTEREVIDENCE
"The ultimate distortion appeared in this morning's New York Times editorial, which speaks of the agency 'having to be stopped from illegal ... murders.' This distortion of the reality must be corrected." *Letter from William J. Casey to members of the House and Senate Intelligence Committees October 25, 1984*	"Selective Use of Violence for Propagandistic Effects: It is possible to neutralize carefully selected and planned targets, such as court judges, *mesta* judges, police and State Security officials ... [P]rofessional criminals will be hired to carry out specific selective 'jobs' ... Specific tasks will be assigned to others ... in order to bring about uprisings or shootings, which will cause the death of one or more per-

Casey

sons, who would become the martyrs. . . ."
"Psychological Operations and Guerrilla Warfare," CIA Manual for Nicaraguan contras, Fall, 1983

"The Committee was told that all CIA officers should have known about the Executive Order's ban on assassination and about the Boland Amendment but some did not. . . . The incident of the manual illustrates once again to a majority of the Committee that the CIA did not have adequate command and control of the entire Nicaraguan covert action."
House Intelligence Committee, Press Release December 5, 1984

"It is CIA policy not to condone, participate in, or promote by instruction or any other means, murder, the use of torture, or any other gross violation of human rights."
Report of the Senate Committee on Intelligence October 5, 1984

"Insurgent incidents" over the previous four months included "attacks by small guerrilla bands on individual Sandinista soldiers and the assassination of minor government officials and a Cuban advisor."
Weekly Intelligence Summary prepared by Defense Intelligence Agency July 16, 1982

"It's not hard to tell as we look around the world, who are the terrorists and who are the freedom fighters. . . . The contras in Nicaragua do not blow up school buses or hold mass executions of civilians."
George Shultz, June 24, 1983, entered in Congressional Record October 3, 1984

"They [the contras] have attacked civilians indiscriminately; they have tortured and mutilated prisoners; they have murdered those placed *hors de combat* by their wounds; they have taken hostages; and they have committed outrages against personal dignity."
"Violations of the Laws of War by Both Sides in Nicaragua 1981-1985," Americas Watch March 1985

"On December 4, 1984, a contra task force ambushed a truck carrying volunteer coffeepickers . . . near Telpaneca in the Department of Madriz. Twenty-one civilians, including a mother and her 5 year old child who had hitched a ride, were killed . . . the contras, some 150-300, advanced on the truck, firing . . . Next they set the truck on fire with gasoline . . . From where Roger Briones lay, 'I could hear the cries and laments of those who were burning alive.'"

"Attacks By the Nicaraguan 'Contras' on the Civilian Population of Nicaragua," Report by Reed Brody, Former Assistant Attorney General of the State of New York March 1985

"One source said that in early April, Casey was asked [in House Intelligence Committee secret meetings] about an NBC News report on a contra attack against a Nicaraguan farm cooperative, and the CIA director denied that the attack was carried out by CIA-backed forces . . . a congressional investigator later [after Casey's testimony] uncovered a CIA 'after-action' report on the assault . . . the CIA maintains such reports only on actions in which it is involved."

Associated Press August 19, 1983

". . . FDN has engaged repeatedly in kidnappings, torture and murder of unarmed civilians, mostly in villages and farm cooperatives. . . ."

Americas Watch Report April 1984

"The FDN is believed to consist of activists from . . . the following organizations: — 15 September Legion . . . a "Somocista" group founded by Bermudez and Herberto Sanchez. . . . It is a terrorist group comprised of a small number of commandos believed to be operating out of Honduras."

Weekly Intelligence summary prepared by Defense Intelligence Agency July 16, 1982

"The freedom fighters are peasants, farmers, shopkeepers, and vendors. Their leaders are without exception men who opposed Somoza."

Langhorne Motley, before the Western Hemisphere Subcommittee January 29, 1985

"Former national guardsman—mostly non-commissioned officers—lead many of these [contra] guerrilla units."

Thomas Enders before the Senate Foreign Relations Committee April 12, 1983

"[A]lmost all of the top [contra] commanders are former National Guard officers."

New York Times March 24, 1985

V. THE ALLEGED ARMS BUILDUP

ISSUE: The charters of the Organization of American States (OAS) and of the United Nations (UN) stipulate that members of these organizations cannot use military force as an instrument of foreign policy except in instances of individual and collective self-defense. The Reagan Administration cites the commitment to collective self-defense in the charters as justification for its intervention against Nicaragua. The Administration claims that the Nicaraguan military "buildup" constitutes a threat of intervention and of "export of revolution" to neighboring Central American states. Does the Reagan Administration accurately portray the extent and the nature of the Nicaraguan military "buildup?"

ADMINISTRATION POSITION	COUNTEREVIDENCE

"The Sandinistas have been attacking their neighbors through armed subversion since August of 1979. Countering this by supporting Nicaraguan freedom fighters is essentially acting in self-defense and is certainly consistent with the United Nations and OAS Charter provisions for individual and collective security."

President Reagan, at the Western Hemisphere Legislative Leaders Forum January 24, 1985

"The force that the Nicaraguans could put into Honduras would not therefore be large enough to make it very likely that the Nicaraguans would risk an invasion out of any motive other than desperation. . . . In addition to the exile forces operating from Honduras and Costa Rica, Nicaragua also feels threatened by the direct U.S. military involvement in the area. . . . For a country that has been invaded by the United States on nine different occasions, a U.S. presence of close to 5,000 men in Honduras is sufficient cause for concern."

"Central America: The Deepening Conflict," Report of A Congressional Study Mission August 29, 1984

"I do not believe they [the Nicaraguans] intend to do it [attack neighboring countries]. I don't believe they would do it for the obvious reasons that they would have at this juncture little to gain for the risks incurred . . . It would bring the region down on them."

General Paul Gorman before the Senate Armed Services Committee February 23, 1984

"The disparity between the Sandinista armed forces and those of its neighbors is unwarranted by any stretch of the imagination and seriously threatens regional balance and stability."

Nestor Sanchez, Deputy Assistant Secretary of Defense of Inter-American Affairs, before the House Subcommittee on Western Hemisphere Affairs March 1, 1983

". . . the armed forces of the two nations have different areas of strength and weakness but the overall effect is a balance of force in the realm of more sophisticated armaments. While the Honduran Air Force is markedly superior to Nicaragua's, the Nicaragua air defenses offset this advantage. And while the Nicaraguans may have a slight advantage in heavy armored vehicles (tanks), this equipment is of limited effectiveness in the region and of inferior quality. The projected U.S.-

financed arms buildup to Honduras could tip this balance. . . ."
Lt. Col. John Buchanan, USMC (ret.) before the House Subcommittee on Inter-American Affairs, September 21, 1982

"In less than five years the Sandinistas have built the largest and best equipped military force in Central America . . . a mobility and firepower capacity unmatched in the region."
"Nicaragua's Military Build-up and Support for Central American Subversion" by Department of State/Department of Defense July 18, 1984

Air Force Craft in Central America

	Combat Aircraft
El Salvador	59
Guatemala	16
Honduras	30
Nicaragua	12

International Institute for Strategic Studies, 1984 figures. Cited in New York Times November 8, 1984

Nicaragua—The Military Buildup Since July 1979
Total tanks: 150
Total fixed wing aircraft: 45
Figures released by The Department of Defense November 15, 1984

Nicaragua—The Military Balance

Total tanks: 70
Total fixed wing aircraft: 19
Figures released by the International Institute for Strategic Studies, London Fall, 1984

"The current—and growing—138,000 man armed force in Nicaragua stands in sharp contrast to the 33,000 man armed force in El Salvador . . ."
Nestor Sanchez, before the Subcommittee on Western Hemisphere Affairs March 1, 1983

"According to the Embassy, at the time of the delegation's visit [August/September 1983] there were 22,000 men in the regular army, navy and air force, 20,000 reservists; and 80,000 militia, for a total of 122,000 . . . The militia are not well-trained . . . are good only for defense and should not be counted as part of an offensive army. Therefore, the delegation estimates that the Nicaraguans could field about 40,000 well-trained men."
"Central America: The Deepening Conflict" Congressional Study Report August 29, 1984

"We see 36 military bases and garrisons in Nicaragua now under construction or completed. By contrast in neighboring Honduras no new military bases are

"One of the (36) sites mentioned, Tipitapa, has been visited by a number of Western journalists; the construction in question is that of a very large sugar plant . . ."
Jacobson Report, commissioned by the State Department • June 1984

ADMINISTRATION POSITION	COUNTEREVIDENCE
being considered."	"... many [military garrisons] ... are so small that the Honduran pilots will have difficulty locating them. For example, the 'military garrison' near Somoto, where I stopped for lunch, was comprised of two small buildings and a one-vehicle lean-to maintenance shed." *Lt. Col. John Buchanan, USMC (ret.) before the House Subcommittee on Inter-American Affairs September 21, 1982* "There were two open tin-roofed sheds on each side of the custom house which were empty except for piles of dirt and debris on the floors. From their appearance these sheds had not been used for a very long time. These sheds were listed in the [Department of Defense/State Department] 'Green Book' as 'auxiliary buildings' just as the run down guard hut was noted as a military barracks ... My impression after visiting the Potosi area and then later seeing DOD aerial photos taken before my visit was that the DOD claims and photos did not reflect the reality of what I saw on the ground with first hand observation." *"Report on Military and Political Situation in Central America" by Lt. Col. Edward L. King, USA (Ret.) September 11, 1984*
"First of all, we need to read and listen to what people say, and I think a lot of people made a mistake when they did not read 'Mein Kampf.' Hitler laid it all out. Nobody believed it. The Communist leaders regularly say what their objectives are. They do not conceal them, nor does the Government of Nicaragua conceal that what it wants is 'a revolution without frontiers.'" *Secretary of State George P. Shultz, before the Senate Foreign Relations Committee August 4, 1983*	"The phrase 'revolution without frontiers,' which the Reagan administration has frequently used to describe and condemn Nicaraguan foreign policy, apparently has never been used by the Nicaraguans but instead 'originated inside the Beltway,' Rep. Edward J. Markey (D-Mass.) charged yesterday ... In other words, Markey said, "they don't have a citation. The credibility of the administration is seriously diminished when they disseminate this phrase that has such incendiary overtones." *Washington Post October 4, 1983*

ISSUE: Does the Reagan Administration accurately describe the extent and nature of Soviet and Cuban military involvement in Nicaragua?

ADMINISTRATION POSITION	COUNTEREVIDENCE
"Soviet bloc ship deliveries to Nicaragua over the past three years have destabilized the military balance in Central America . . . The massive military buildup in Nicaragua intimidates neighboring Costa Rica, Honduras, and El Salvador . . . Nicaragua's military equipment inventory now includes about 150 T55 tanks and PT76 amphibious tanks . . ." *Nestor Sanchez, before the House Subcommittee on Western Hemisphere Affairs February 28, 1985*	"the limited amounts of truly modern equipment acquired by the Sandinistas . . . came from Western Europe, not the Eastern bloc." *Jacobsen Report June 1984* According to Lt. Col. John Buchanan, USMC (ret.), "the might of the Nicaraguan air force is infinitesimal . . . the much vaunted threat of the Soviet-built T-55 tanks in Nicaragua is really a hollow threat." Buchanan cited the tanks "terrible mechanical performance" and the rugged terrain in the area, which he said "is totally unsuited to tank warfare." *New York Times April 27, 1983*
"Nicaragua today has created the biggest military force in all of Central America and large parts of South America . . . armed with Soviet weapons that consist of heavy-duty tanks, an air force, helicopter gunships, fighter planes, bombers, and so forth . . ." *President Reagan, Remarks to the press April 14, 1983*	"The chairman of the largest anti-Sandinista rebel force [Enrique Bermudez] says his troops have seen little evidence of the major buildup of Soviet arms in Nicaragua that Reagan Administration officials have described" *New York Times November 22, 1984* "The overall buildup is primarily defense oriented, and much of the recent effort has been devoted to improving counter insurgency capabilities." *U.S. Intelligence Report prepared in late 1984, cited in Wall Street Journal April 3, 1985*
". . . the Committee inquired about statements by Administration officials on March 10, 1982 which reportedly indicated that "detailed outlines" of Soviet and Cuban plans in Central America had been obtained." *Staff Report, Subcommittee on Oversight and Evaluation, House Select Committee on Intelligence Sept. 22, 1982*	"In a written response, CIA clarified that . . . no 'detailed plan' had been obtained." *Staff Report, Subcommittee on Oversight and Evaluation, Permanent Select Committee on Intelligence Sept. 22, 1982*

VI. THE WAR POWERS ACT

ISSUE: The War Powers Act prohibits the President from introducing U.S. Armed Forces into hostilities or into territory, airspace or waters of a foreign nation without submitting notification to Congress within 48 hours. Has the Reagan Administration adhered to this procedure, as it has claimed in testimony before Congress?

ADMINISTRATION POSITION	COUNTEREVIDENCE
Mr. Reid: "Will they [U.S. forces] enter Nicaraguan territory, airspace, or Nicaraguan waters? *Mr. Motley:* No, sir, they will not. They will stay back a very good distance so that they can't inadvertently stumble into it." *Langhorne Motley, before the Subcommittee on Human Rights and International Organizations August 3, 1983*	"U.S. troops engaged in exercises in Honduras have conducted operations including simulated helicopter assault missions in close proximity to . . . the Nicaraguan Army. . . . During an exercise in January, 1984, a U.S. Army helicopter was shot down over the Honduran/Nicaraguan border after it had reportedly been blown off course some 20 miles. . ." *"U.S. Policy in Central America: Against the Law?" Report by the Arms Control and Foreign Policy Caucus • September 11, 1984* "For the fourth consecutive day, a United States reconnaissance aircraft shattered the sound barrier in violation of Nicaragua's airspace, Defense Ministry officials said." *Washington Post November 12, 1984*
"Those maneuvers . . . are not going to put Americans in any reasonable proximity to the Honduran-Nicaraguan border. *President Reagan Washington Post July 27, 1983*	"Since November 1983 . . . the 46th Combat Engineers had been independently digging anti-tank ditches in the Choluteca area, as close as 5 kilometers to the Nicaragua-Honduras border." *"GAO Responses To Questions In November 14, 1983, Letter," Report by the General Accounting Office*
"And we are not engaging in acts of war against anybody." *Jeane Kirkpatrick, U.S. Ambassador to the United Nations, before the Senate Committee on Foreign Relations March 1, 1982*	"It [the mining of Nicaraguan harbors] is an act of war. For the life of me I don't see how we're going to explain it." *Letter from Sen. Barry M. Goldwater, chair of the Senate Intelligence Committee to William J. Casey, Director CIA April 9, 1984*

EL SALVADOR

The Reagan Administration has been required to testify before Congress in order to send larger doses of military and economic aid to El Salvador. During hearings, the Administration has assured Congress that it has faithfully executed the law on various issues effecting U.S. assistance. These issues can be grouped under the following four categories:

I. PROGRESS OF GOVERNMENT REFORMS

The *International Security and Development and Cooperation Act of 1981* specified that the President could release military assistance to El Salvador only after he certified every six months that several conditions had been met. Three of the most significant conditions were that the El Salvador government (a) had complied with internationally recognized human rights; (b) had gained control over the armed forces which had abused human rights; (c) had made progress on implementing a land reform program. Amid great controversy, the Administration certified military aid to El Salvador four times, the first time in early 1982, the last in mid-1983. President Reagan pocket-vetoed the certification requirement in November 1983. During and after the certification period, the Administration appears to have misled Congress as to the status of reforms by the Salvadoran government.

II. HUMAN RIGHTS

The *Foreign Assistance Act of 1974* prohibits the U.S. from providing military assistance to a government "which engages in a consistent pattern of gross violations of internationally recognized human rights." The *1949 Geneva Conventions* on the protection of civilians obligates the U.S. to insure respect of the conventions by other governments. These two laws, along with other international human rights standards and accords, appear to have been violated by Salvadoran government forces. Indiscriminate bombings by the Salvadoran air force, political murders committed by death squads closely linked to government security forces, and regular patrols and ground sweeps by the Salvadoran military— which include U.S.-trained battalions—have grossly violated the rights of El Salvador's civilian population.

III. HOSTILITIES ENDANGERING U.S. PERSONNEL

The *Arms Export Control Act* obligates the President to notify Congress whenever U.S. military personnel are seriously endangered. The *War Powers Act of 1973* requires the President to report to Congress whenever U.S. forces are engaged in fighting, or are introduced into areas where hostilities are occuring or might occur. It further requires the President to remove the troops after 60 days—or 90 days with an extension—unless Congress authorizes their continued presence, in light of the report on hostilities. Despite assurances by Reagan officials that such instances would be thoroughly reported to Congress, the record documented here indicates that Congress has been left unaware of numerous instances of hostilities against U.S. personnel in El Salvador.

IV. APPROPRIATIONS

Although the issues raised under this section do not directly violate any specific laws per se, they do address the crucial issue of trust between the Executive and Congress, and whether or not the Executive has properly informed Congress as to the purpose and use of funds provided to El Salvador. Specifically, this section asks whether or not the Administration deceived Congress when it denied in testimony that it was considering sending supplemental money to El Salvador in the spring of 1984, and if the White House has generally misled Congress by exaggerating the "economic and social development" component of all U.S. aid provided to El Salvador over the past five years.

I. PROGRESS OF GOVERNMENT REFORMS

ISSUE: Did the Government of El Salvador, as the Reagan Administration certified to Congress, make a concerted effort to comply with international standards of human rights between July 1981 and June 1983?

ADMINISTRATION POSITION	COUNTEREVIDENCE

"[T]he Government of El Salvador is making a concerted and significant effort to comply with internationally recognized human rights" and "is achieving substantial control over all elements of its armed forces, so as to bring to an end the indiscriminate torture and murder of Salvadoran citizens."

President Ronald Reagan, Presidential Certification on El Salvador, January 28, 1982. Certified every six months thereafter, ending in June 1983.

Reagan

"[W]e cannot argue that violence is down since the first certification."

Craig Johnstone, Assistant Secretary of State for Central America, in memorandum entitled "Second certification on Human Rights in El Salvador." June 12, 1982

13,353 Salvadorans were murdered by the army, security forces and paramilitary groups during the year preceding the president's first certification.

Socorro Juridico, the Legal Aid Office of the Archdiocese of El Salvador, in compilation of weekly reports on murders of civilians by government forces January to December 1981

2,527 civilians were murdered by government forces and paramilitary groups aligned with government forces during the first six months of 1983. This is an increase from the 2,340 murders during the last six months of 1982.

Tutela Legal [successor to Socorro Juridico], the Human Rights Office of the Archdiocese of El Salvador, in compilation of weekly reports on murders of civilians by government forces July 1982 to June 1983

The International Committee of the Red Cross "has seen a continuing deterioration in the treatment of detainees since April. Perhaps as many as ninety percent of detainees are being tortured during interrogation. Torture is being employed in some of the formerly more humane centers, such as those run by the National Police."

International Red Cross cable November 1983

"According to unclassified cables from the U.S. Embassy in San Salvador 1,072 civilians died in political violence

between December 16 and June 15, the latest six-month period available. That is a 12 percent increase over the 961 civilians killed the previous six months."
The Baltimore Sun
July 7, 1983

ISSUE: The Reagan Administration certified four times to Congress that the Government of El Salvador was "achieving substantial control over all elements of its armed forces, as to bring to an end the indiscriminate torture and murder of Salvadoran citizens." Has the Salvadoran government seriously disciplined members of its armed forces who commit human rights abuses?

ADMINISTRATION POSITION	COUNTEREVIDENCE

Mr. Bonker: It is my understanding not one person has been tried or convicted of terrorist activity or human rights violations.

Mr. Abrams: Several hundred officers have been dismissed from the Armed Forces or have been jailed.
Elliot Abrams, Assistant Secretary of State for Human Rights and Humanitarian Affairs, before the House Committee on Foreign Affairs July 29, 1982

The Salvadoran military has "transferred, retired, cashiered or punished 1,000 officers and men for various abuses of authority."
Thomas Enders, Assistant Secretary of State for Inter-American Affairs, during the First Presidential Certification on El Salvador before the House Committee on Foreign Affairs February 2, 1982

A cable by the U.S. embassy in San Salvador reports that only 12 officers had been disciplined during the period January 1, 1982 to mid-July 1982. "To the best of our knowledge these are the *first* instances where the Ministry of Defense has reported officers have been arrested or investigated [emphasis added]."
Deane Hinton, U.S. Ambassador to El Salvador, in embassy cable sent in July 1982

"[T]he Salvadoran government has not yet demonstrated that it has the will and the capacity to bring to justice those responsible for mass murder and other gross violations of human rights. No member of the regular armed forces of El Salvador has yet been punished criminally for a violation of human rights against other Salvadorans in more than five years. Nor has there been a single criminal conviction for non-uniformed death squads.

As yet, in our view, the government of President Duarte has failed to demonstrate that it can exercise effective authority over all elements of the armed forces."
Aryeh Neier, Vice Chairman, Americas Watch, before the Subcommittee on Western Hemisphere Affairs of the House Committee on Foreign Affairs January 31, 1985

ISSUE: The Reagan Administration certified four times to Congress that the Government of El Salvador was "making continued progress in implementing essential economic and political reform, including the land reform program." Even after the certification requirement was vetoed by President Reagan, Administration officials continued to praise the agrarian program. The most significant aspect of the reform—Phase III—was cancelled by the Salvadoran legislature in June 1984. Did the Reagan Administration deceive Congress as to the actual progress of the land reform program?

ADMINISTRATION POSITION	COUNTEREVIDENCE
The Government of El Salvador "is making continued progress in implementing . . . the land reform program." *Section 728 of the Foreign Assistance Act, certified by the Reagan Administration before the House Committee on Foreign Affairs • June 2, 1982*	"[T]here has been extensive regression, not 'continued progress' in the land reform." *Roy Prosterman, advisor to AIFLD and architect of El Salvador's land reform, in the New Republic August 9, 1982*
The agrarian program "is one of the major stories of the past four years . . . [P]roductivity on reformed lands has reached levels comparable to the traditional sector." *Langhorne Motley, Assistant Secretary of State for Inter-American Affairs, before the House Foreign Affairs Committee January 26, 1984*	Farm cooperatives created under the first phase of the reform program "had massive capital debt, no working capital, large tracts of land that were nonproductive, substantially larger labor forces than needed to operate the units, and weak management." The future of these cooperatives "seems bleak without further substantial reforms. Most are not producing sufficient income to be viable organizations." *"Agrarian Reform in El Salvador, A Report On Its Status," the Inspector General, U.S. Agency for International Development (USAID) January 18, 1984*
"[T]he best available data indicates that at least 85 per cent and probably more than 90 per cent of applicants [of the Phase III program] are working their land without interference." *Langhorne Motley, before the House Foreign Affairs Committee January 26, 1984*	"[L]ess than one-half (about 50,000 out of an estimated 117,000) of the individuals eligible for property under Phase III had filed applications to purchase the land. And about one-third of the applicants filed did not result in the applicants working the land. They were not working the land because they had been threatened, evicted or had disappeared." *"Agrarian Reform in El Salvador, A Report On Its Status," USAID • January 18, 1984*

II. HUMAN RIGHTS

ISSUE: The Reagan Administration has absolved the Salvadoran government of responsibility for civilian killings by so-called 'death squads' by characterizing them as being composed of extremists operating outside of the government's military and security forces. Are the death squads really fringe elements which function beyond the control of government forces?

ADMINISTRATION POSITION	COUNTEREVIDENCE
"In other words, there is no campaign directed out of a headquarters somewhere, or several headquarters somewhere, in the government, associated with the government, to eliminate the following numbers of people." *Thomas Enders, before the Subcommittees on Human Rights and International Organizations and on Western Hemisphere Affairs of the House Committee on Foreign Affairs* *February 4, 1983*	"It is a grievous error to believe that the forces of the extreme right, or the so-called 'Death Squads,' operate independently of the security forces. The simple truth is that 'Los Escuardrones de la Muerte' are made up of members of the security forces and acts of terrorism . . . are planned by high-ranking military officers . . ." *Salvadoran Army Captain Ricardo Fiallos, a 16 year army veteran, before the Foreign Operations Subcommittee of the House Appropriations Committee* *April 29, 1981*
"It is not an organized movement. It is not a structure that has a headquarters that gives commands. It is a spontaneous phenomenon, not, as far as we can see, orchestrated . . . It is a lot of people who are taking the law into their own hands and are committing injustices." *Thomas Enders, before the Senate Foreign Relations Committee* *February 2, 1983*	"All of the death squads are related to the army or paramilitary." *Salvadoran President Alvaro Magana in March 1982, as quoted by Representative Gerry Studds before the Subcommittees on Human Rights and International Organizations and on Western Hemisphere Affairs of the House Committee on Foreign Affairs* *August 3, 1983* "Death squad activities, as well as other abuses provoked by extreme rightwing officers, or their associates, have originated in the Salvadoran security services, including the National Police, National Guard and Treasury Police." *"Recent Political Violence In El Salvador," a report of the Senate Select Committee on Intelligence* *October 5, 1984*

Enders

ADMINISTRATION POSITION	COUNTEREVIDENCE
Death squad activities "are not condoned by most of the military or security force leadership nor most of the mid and junior level officers in the field." *Thomas Enders, before the Senate Foreign Relations Committee February 2, 1983*	"Numerous Salvadoran officials in the military and security forces as well as other official organizations have been involved in encouraging or conducting death squad activities or other violent human rights abuses. This has included many middle-level officers and a few high-ranking officials; a large number of low-level personnel have also been involved." *"Recent Political Violence In El Salvador," a report of the Senate Select Committee on Intelligence October 5, 1984*
"(W)e don't know who the death squads are." *Elliot Abrams, before the Subcommittees on Human Rights and International Organizations and on Western Hemisphere Affairs of the House Committee on Foreign Affairs August 3, 1983*	"A number of prominent Salvadorans have supported, directed or engaged in death squad activities in addition to having encouraged other violent human rights abuses. This has included officials in the civilian government, representatives of the private sector organizations, and various individuals associated with the traditional oligarchy of that country." *"Recent Political Violence In El Salvador," a report of the Senate Select Committee on Intelligence October 5, 1984*

ISSUE: Has the Salvadoran military conducted indiscriminate bombings upon the civilian population?

ADMINISTRATION POSITION	COUNTEREVIDENCE
"[T]he Army and Air Force do not conduct indiscriminate bombings or artillery shellings . . . systematic or frequent bombings have not occurred. We have no evidence that violence has been used gratuitously against civilians . . ." *State Department response to question submitted by Michael Barnes, Chairman of the Western Hemisphere Subcommittee of the House Foreign Affairs Committee August 22, 1984*	"Thousands of noncombatants are being killed in indiscriminate attacks by bombardment from the air, shelling, and ground sweeps. Thousands more are being wounded . . . the armed forces of El Salvador, ground and air, are engaged in indiscriminate attacks upon the civilian population in conflict zones—particularly in guerrilla controlled zones—of El Salvador." *Americas Watch, Report on Human Rights in El Salvador August 1984*

ADMINISTRATION POSITION	COUNTEREVIDENCE
	"The Salvadoran Air Force has increased indiscriminate bombing raids in conflictive and guerrilla-held zones, according to residents and recently displaced people from the Cuscalatan and Cabanas provinces." *Christian Science Monitor* *April 6, 1984* "President Jose Napoleon Duarte announced today he has tightened rules for bombing by the Salvadoran Air Force in an effort to reduce civilian casualties . . . Raids by U.S.-supplied A37 Dragonfly jets dropping 500- and 750-pound iron bombs have been a major source of complaint by human rights groups . . . By taking steps to prevent civilian casualties, the government seemed to indirectly acknowledge that at least some of the allegations [of civilians being bombed] are true." *Washington Post* *Sept. 13, 1984*

ISSUE: Have U.S.-trained military battalions—particularly the Atlacatl battalion—committed significant human rights abuses against Salvadoran civilians?

ADMINISTRATION POSITION	COUNTEREVIDENCE
"The first quick-reaction battalion trained by U.S. instructors—the Atlacatl Battalion—has achieved a commendable combat record not only for its tactical capability in fighting the guerrillas but also for its humane treatment of the people." *Nestor Sanchez, Deputy Assistant Secretary of Defense for Inter-American Affairs, before the House Committee on Foreign Affairs* *June 2, 1982* "We do not have documented [human rights] charges against them in a	"(I)n the Salvadoran countryside, regular Army as well as the new U.S.-trained rapid deployment forces, the Atlacatl, Ramon Belloso, and Antonal brigades are frequently cited as responsible for massive killings of noncombatant civilians." *Amnesty International, "Assigning Responsibility for Human Rights Abuses: El Salvador's Military and Security Units"* *September 1982*

significant way. We simply do not have evidence that these American-trained battalions have engaged in significant human rights abuses that have come to our attention. As you know, we spend a lot of time trying to monitor this."

Thomas Enders, before the House Committee on Appropriations March 16, 1983

"(I)t is clear that a massacre of major proportions occurred here [in Mozote] last month . . . peasants said that . . . their relatives and friends had been killed by Government soldiers of the Atlacatl Battalion in a sweep in December."

"The villagers have compiled a list of 733 peasants, mostly children, women and old people, who they say were murdered by the Government soldiers. The Human Rights Commission of El Salvador, which works with the Roman Catholic Church, puts the number at 926."

New York Times January 27, 1982

"[T]he signs of the slaughter were everywhere: charred and scattered bits of clothing, shoes and schoolbooks . . .

The Tenango villagers said the elite, U.S-trained *Brigada Infanteria Reaccionara Immediata Atlacatl* had committed the atrocities. As evidence, they showed us chalk graffiti marks left by the soldiers congratulating the Atlacatl Brigade on its second anniversary . . .

I asked a rebel commander for a final tally of guerrilla casualties. Since the Army went into Guazapa, he said, it had managed to kill 100 civilians and wound 20 guerrillas—and eliminate all of five rebels."

Newsweek April 25, 1983

Local peasants "say that between July 18 and July 22, Salvadoran Army troops killed 68 undefended residents of this village [Los Llanitos] and several neighboring communities . . . a report last month by the Salvadoran Roman Catholic Church Legal Aid Office supported their charges."

A "Salvadoran officer close to the high command said the units involved in the operation in July were the Atlacatl battalion, the First Infantry Bri-

gade and the Fifth Military Detachment based in the town of Cojutepeque."
New York Times
September 9, 1984

III. HOSTILITIES ENDANGERING U.S. PERSONNEL

ISSUE: Has the President violated the War Powers Act by failing to report to Congress when U.S. forces in El Salvador have been introduced "into hostilities or into a situation where imminent involvement in hostilities is clearly indicated by the circumstances?"

ADMINISTRATION POSITION	COUNTEREVIDENCE
"U.S. military personnel will not go on land or sea patrols, fly in helicopters on combat missions, or be otherwise placed or place themselves in a situation where combat is likely." *Department of Defense response to a question submitted by Senator Zorinsky, printed in text of a hearing before the Senate Foreign Relations Committee* *February 2, 1983* "Our representatives . . . are not to be introduced into areas of imminent hostilities." *Thomas Enders, before the Subcommittees on Human Rights and International Organizations and on Western Hemisphere Affairs of the House Committee on Foreign Affairs* *February 4, 1983* "We are not putting our people in a situation where there is any imminent danger of hostilities." *Langhorne Motley, before the House Subcommittee on Western Hemisphere Affairs* *May 2, 1984*	"U.S. military advisors in El Salvador have come under fire on at least eight separate incidents." "U.S. Army pilots have been flying reconnaissance missions from Honduras and Panama over Salvadoran battlefields, providing information to combat operations of the Salvadoran Army. This information at times has been reported to include coordinates of rebel positions and previous placement of Salvadoran artillery shells, to help Salvadoran units 'spot' their fire accurately." "U.S. Navy ships have participated in naval interdiction activities in the Gulf of Fonseca, locating and tracking possibly hostile ships for interdiction by the Salvadoran Navy." *"U.S. Policy in Central America: Against the Law?," report by the Arms Control and Foreign Policy Caucus* *September 11, 1984*

ISSUE: Has the Reagan Administration complied with section 21 (c)(2) of the Arms Export Control Act which requires the President to notify Congress "within 48 hours of, or a change in the status of significant hostilities . . . which may endanger American lives or property involving a country which United States personnel are performing defense services . . ."?

ADMINISTRATION POSITION	COUNTEREVIDENCE
"This Administration is fully committed to the letter and purpose of section 21 (c)(2) and to providing the Congress with all the information it may require concerning El Salvador . . . I assure you that this Administration will comply fully with the requirements of section 21 (c)(2) in any future situation in which they apply. In particular, should the violence in El Salvador increase in the future, we will consult with the Department of State and insure the timely preparation and transmittal of a report to Congress whenever one is required by section 21 (c)(2)."	"More important, with respect to section 21 (c)(2) compliance, was the guerrilla's January 27, 1982 raid on Ilopango, the main Salvadoran air force base . . . Among the aircraft destroyed or damaged were four U.S. Army helicopters leased to the Salvadoran government. Additionally, there were U.S. trainers deployed to the base . . . Despite these property losses and the possible endangering of U.S. personnel . . . no report was filed. We believe a report should have been filed."

Letter from Frank Carlucci, Undersecretary of Defense for Policy Planning, to Charles Percy, Chairman of the Senate Foreign Relations Committee March 13, 1981

"Applicability of Certain U.S. Laws that Pertain to U.S. Military Involvement in El Salvador," report by the General Accounting Office (GAO) July 27, 1982

"Critics charge that the minimum of eight incidents in El Salvador in which U.S. military advisers have been fired on by rebel forces constitute 'significant hostilities' that 'may endanger American lives,' and that failure to report these incidents to Congress violates section 21 (c)(2)."

"U.S. Policy in Central America: Against the Law?," a report by the Arms Control and Foreign Policy Caucus September 11, 1984

"[A] report is to be made to Congress if a military assistance person is harmed or killed in an incident. There is a regular form for that. It is section 21 of the Arms Export Control Act . . . We would certainly intend to report under that."

Thomas Enders, before the Subcommittees on Human Rights and International Organizations and on Western Hemisphere Affairs of the House Committee on Foreign Affairs •February 4, 1983

ISSUE: Was the State Department telling the truth when it filed monthly reports to Congress from April 1981 to October 1982 stating that there had been no attacks on U.S. military advisors?

ADMINISTRATION POSITION	COUNTEREVIDENCE
"There were no security incidents involving U.S. personnel." *Concluding statement on the security situation in El Salvador in monthly State Department report to Congress. Statement was included in 15 of the 18 reports filed. Only 3 security incidents were reported during this period April 1981 to October 1982*	"All of my men have been shot at." *Special Forces sargeant,* *U.S. News & World Report* *October 11, 1982* "HFP [hostile fire pay] was paid for 97 of the 123 total person months" to U.S. advisors in El Salvador between January 1981 and March 1982. [To receive hostile fire pay, advisors signed a statement saying "I was subjected to hostile fire" during the month in which they were applying]. *"Applicability of Certain U.S. Laws that Pertain to U.S. Military Involvement in El Salvador," report by the GAO July 27, 1982*

IV. APPROPRIATIONS

ISSUE: During the spring of 1984 President Reagan asked Congress to approve normal requests for military aid appropriations to El Salvador. At that time, Administration officials—including Secretary of Defense Weinberger—denied that the White House was considering approval of contingency funds if congressional monies were withheld. Despite these denials, the White House subsequently bypassed Congress and sent $32 million to El Salvador. Did the Reagan Administration deceive Congress by denying it was contemplating to dispatch such contingency money?

ADMINISTRATION POSITION	COUNTEREVIDENCE
Mr. Barnes: Has the administration approved the provision of additional military assistance to El Salvador beyond assistance that the Congress has authorized and appropriated? *Secretary Weinberger:* We can't do that under any circumstances for any country. *Mr. Barnes:* There are provisions in the law that permit the advancement of funds if	"An assessment of short-term military needs indicates that the government of El Salvador will need additional defense articles, services and training before an FY84 supplemental can be approved. Therefore, if necessary, action may be taken to provide requisite resources under the provisions of Section 21(d) of the Arms Export Control Act." *National Security Decision Document 124, signed by President Reagan in February, 1984*

you anticipate for example, a supplemental. Has any decision been made to do that?

Secretary Weinberger: Not to my knowledge. Whatever is done has been reported in the budget and in the supplemental the needs are very great. They are entirely within the laws that govern this matter and I am not aware of any recommendations or any allocations—

Mr. Barnes: Would you have your staff check on that and give us an answer, because I have information that is contrary to your understanding.

Caspar Weinberger, before the House Committee on Foreign Affairs February 9, 1984

ISSUE: During the past five years the U.S. has provided $1.7 billion in aid to El Salvador. Administration officials have continually emphasized that social and economic development aid outstrips military aid by a three to one margin. Has the Reagan Administration misled Congress as to the actual purpose and use of U.S. aid to El Salvador?

"By any measure, the assistance package we are proposing is heavily weighted toward economic aid. Taking both the supplemental and the fiscal year 1984 requests, proposed economic assistance is more than three times larger than military assistance."

Thomas Enders, before the Subcommittee on Western Hemisphere Affairs of the Senate Foreign Relations Committee March 14, 1983

"The Administration repeatedly asserts that 'by a three to one margin,' aid is allocated to 'economic and social development' rather than a 'military solution' to El Salvador's civil war. . . in fact the opposite is closer to the truth."

The Administration "has provided insufficient, misleading and in some cases false information to Congress. . . Aid for reform and development. . . accounts for only *15 percent* of total U.S. funding for El Salvador over the past five years. Direct war-related aid . . . represents 30 percent of our

"Clearly, the President is not 'militarizing' his approach— as some have alleged. The economic aid recommended for the next five years exceeds the military aid."

Fred Ikle, before the Senate
Foreign Relations Committee
March 20, 1984

total aid program. . . Indirect war-related aid, which addresses needs arising from the civil war and in some cases actually assists in the prosecution of the war, accounts for the largest single category of U.S. funds over the past five years: 44 percent of the total U.S. program, or $767 million."

"U.S. Aid to El Salvador," a report to the Arms
Control and Foreign Policy Caucus from Rep.
Jim Leach, Rep. George Miller and
Sen. Mark Hatfield
February 1985

H O N D U R A S

Since 1983, in congressional hearings on the direction of U.S. policy in Honduras and the means used by the Administration to realize its goals, Reagan officials have assured members of Congress (a) that its activities in Honduras are consistent with routine operations, and (b) that the Administration has accurately and fully reported to Congress about the execution of its policy. The testimony has generated several issues that divided into four major categories: (1) proper funding of military construction and military training; (2) collaboration between the CIA and DOD in Honduras; (3) informing Congress about military construction plans; (4) the nature and purpose of military exercises.

I. FUNDING OF MILITARY CONSTRUCTION AND MILITARY TRAINING

The *Military Construction Codification Act* stipulates that military construction projects must be approved by Congress through direct appropriations unless a project costs less than $200,000. A "minor" project may be funded out of the Defense Department's Operation and Maintenance (O & M) Funds. The DOD argues that it has spent money from its O & M fund properly on several facilities it built or improved in Honduras during the Big Pine exercises held in 1983 and 1984. However Congressional studies indicate that the installations built by DOD should not have been funded with O & M funds.

31 USC 1301 (a) of the Defense Department Expenditures guidelines prohibit DOD from spending money on projects other then those for which appropriations are made. The DOD maintains that O & M expenditures during the military exercises in Honduras, which included the joint training of U.S. and Honduran troops, was both legal and in support of necessary training. A GAO report contradicts DOD claims, and asserts that the use of O & M funds for training of Honduran troops is a violation of DOD's legal mandate.

II. COORDINATION OF CIA AND DOD ACTIVITIES
Section 775 of the *Defense Appropriations Act* of 1984 limits funds available to the CIA's operations in Nicaragua to not more than $24 million during fiscal year 1984. The Reagan Administration has assured Congress that the CIA stayed within these restrictions, and specifically that the CIA did not violate the Act by coordinating its activities in Central America with the DOD's operations in Honduras in order to bypass the legislation. Despite Administration officials' claims, a classified report by the General Accounting Office documents that administration officials have left Congress uninformed, and thus misled, as to the actual contact between DOD and the CIA in Honduras.

III. INFORMING CONGRESS ON MILITARY CONSTRUCTION
In October 1983 the Congress passed the *Military Construction Act* of 1984 obligating the DOD to submit to Congress a regional construction plan for Central America before money appropriated by Congress be spent for airfield improvements in Honduras. Although such a report was delivered to Congress on May 8, 1984, the DOD had already begun and, in some cases finished, the construction and improvements of several airstrips in Honduras.

IV. THE NATURE AND PURPOSE OF MILITARY EXERCISES
In 1983 the Reagan Administration began almost continuous joint ground exercises with Honduran troops which often were accompanied by simultaneous naval maneuvers off Central America's coasts. Administration officials have testified before Congress that these exercises are routine and part of a regular schedule. However other Administration officials have contradicted these claims in their reports to the GAO, the press and to members of Congress. While this issue does not directly relate to Congressional legislation

which might restrict such military exercises, it does put into question if the Administration has presented a clear and honest picture to Congress as to its overall policy in Honduras.

I. FUNDING OF MILITARY CONSTRUCTION AND MILITARY TRAINING

ISSUE: Under the Military Construction Codification Act, O & M funds may only be spent on construction projects of less than $200,000. All other military construction must be approved and authorized by Congress. DOD claims that because the airfields, roads, camps and other facilities built in 1983 and 1984 in Honduras were temporary, O & M funds were properly expended and finances were exempt from restrictions of the Military Construction Codification Act. Are the military installations constructed or improved in Honduras temporary or permanent?

ADMINISTRATION POSITION	COUNTEREVIDENCE
". . . I think that what you will find was that, in conjunction with the exercises, temporary facilities were constructed and that there were not any permanent facilities built." *Langhorne Motley, Assistant Secretary of State for Inter-American Affairs, before the House Subcommittee on Western Hemisphere Affairs, May 2, 1984*	"Our own investigations (as recently as late April 1984) show that the majority of these facilities remain in good condition, and in fact continue to be used, both by U.S. and Honduran personnel. Although DOD's March 8, 1984 comment to us state that airfields and facilities 'will deteriorate if not maintained' and that 'Hondurans do not have the resources to maintain,' U.S. Army engineers in Honduras informed GAO auditors that airfields could be used indefinitely with minor amount of maintenance. Facilities remaining in U.S. custody continue to be maintained by U.S. military; those under Honduran control, we have observed are being maintained by the Hondurans." *Report by the General Accounting Office June 22, 1984*
"Facilities built or improved during the exercises were temporary and in direct support of exercise events. They were not designed, and do not meet specifications for long term use." *William H. Taft, Deputy Secretary of Defense, before the House Subcommittee on Military Construction of the House Appropriations Committee May 17, 1984*	"In this instance [Aguacate Airfield], since the runway and water system are virtually permanent, we have created a significant capability in very close proximity to the Nicaraguan border that is not directly related to the exercise." *Unpublished staff report by the House Appropriations Subcommittee on Military Construction February, 1984* ". . . I am reporting to the Senate that the United States has embarked on a

substantial build-up [in Honduras] of permanent and semi-permanent facilities which could be utilized to support contingency operations in Central America . . . at Palmerola . . . the location of the headquarters of joint task force, Alpha, . . . exist sophisticated communications equipment . . . Aguacate is located in Eastern Honduras. There a U.S. engineer battalion has extended a 4300 foot dirt strip to 8,000 feet."

Senator Jim Sasser, statement issued February 8, 1984 following a tour of Honduras.

None of the construction performed by U.S. participants in [Big Pine I or Big Pine II] was permanent. The troop camps are composed of temporary shelters that are either still being used by U.S. personnel or being disposed of through proper channels. . . . The C-130 Assault Runways are definitely not permanent. The runway at San Lorenzo is barely C-130 capable already due to lack of maintenance and severe rutting."

General Paul F. Gorman, Commander of U.S. Southern Command, before the House Subcommittee on Military Construction of the House Committee on Appropriations March 7, 1984

"Although the construction at San Lorenzo is purported to be temporary, the quality and extent of the work is virtually permanent. Sea huts, if properly maintained will last for at least 10 years. The dirt runway, if consistently maintained is usable indefinitely. The Hondurans may, in fact, pave it with their own funds or with U.S. Military Assistance Funds. If the U.S. Military leaves these facilities for Honduran use, the military capability of this location will have been vastly enhanced as a result of this exercise."

Unpublished staff report by the House Appropriations Subcommittee February 1984

The Airfield facility at San Lorenzo was also used by U.S. troops during post-Ahaus Tara II exercises in March and has been used to support the current Grenadero I exercises [April-June 30]. As of April 1984, the airfield at San Lorenzo was still C-130 capable, and had been regraded by Honduran forces. We have been informed that the camp, although unoccupied, is in good condition.

Report by the General Accounting Office June 22, 1984

". . . (San Lorenzo), according to the combat engineer in Honduras, can be expected to last and remain operational for several years and will require little or no maintenance during the dry season and only moderate maintenance during the rainy season in order to remain operational."

Senator Jim Sasser, statement issued February 8, 1984, following tour to Honduras

"The troop shelters, minimal airfield improvements, and other minor projects are temporary in nature, and O & M dollars were appropriately used in funding these activities.

Nestor Sanchez, Deputy Assistant Secretary of Defense, to the House Subcommittee on Military Construction of the House Appropriations Committee March 7, 1984

"The majority of facilities constructed during Ahaus Tara II are substantially less ' temporary ' than many of those [projects] . . . requiring specific funding as public improvements. Consequently, it is our view that the majority of construction activities could not be funded out of O & M as ordinary operational expenses of the joint exercises [in Honduras]. . . ."

Declassified report by the General Accounting Office June 22, 1984

NOTE: *The Military Construction Codification Act allows for the use of O & M funds for military construction projects which cost less than $200,000. By its own accounts, DOD violated this funding restriction. In its regional military construction plan for Central America, submitted to Congress on May 8, 1984, DOD conceded that expenses at four of the nine sites in Honduras exceeded $200,000, as did individual components at three of these four sites.*

ISSUE: *31 USC 1301* (a) of the Defense Department Expenditures guidelines stipulates that appropriations shall be applied only to the projects for which appropriations were allocated, except as otherwise provided by law. It appears that DOD used O & M funds to train Honduran troops during Big Pine II (August 3, 1983 - February 8, 1984) which would be outside DOD's legal mandate. DOD argues that use of O & M funds was permissible because the Honduran army received no formal training, and that any training which occurred was incidental to the exercise. Did Honduran troops receive training from U.S. servicemen without legal sanction?

"There was no formal training of Honduran troops as part of the exercise, however, the U.S. and Honduran forces participated in in-

". . . A GAO field team in Honduras identified 3 types of training conducted by U.S. forces as part of the . . . joint combined exercises [at Palmerola, at Puerto Castilla and San

ADMINISTRATION POSITION	COUNTEREVIDENCE
tegrated exercises which included familiarization and safety orientation at no additional cost to the U.S." *Department of Defense response to questions from the GAO* *March 8, 1984*	Lorenzo]. . . . To the extent that these activities were financed from O & M appropriations as exercise operational expenses, the Department violated 31 USC 1301 (a) which requires funds be applied solely to the purposes for which they were appropriated." *Report by the General Accounting Office* *June 22, 1984*

II. COORDINATION OF CIA AND DOD ACTIVITIES

ISSUE: Section 775 of the Defense Appropriations Act of 1984 states: During fiscal year 1984, not more than $24,000,000 of the funds available to the Central Intelligence Agency, the Department of Defense, or any other agency or entity of the United States involved in intelligence activities may be obligated or expended for purpose of which could have the effect of support directly or indirectly, military or paramilitary operations in Nicaragua by any nation groups, organization, movement or individual. Has there been any contact or coordination between the CIA and the DOD in Honduras which might have enabled the CIA to use DOD's facilities and benefit from DOD's exercise operations, thus bypassing the spending cap imposed by Congress for Fiscal Year 1984?

ADMINISTRATION POSITION	COUNTEREVIDENCE
Rep. Barnes: Will there be any coordination, contact or communication of any kind by the personnel engaged in this exercise [Big Pine II] with either U.S. intelligence personnel or the FDN fighting with Nicaragua? *Mr. Sanchez:* No Sir. *Rep. Barnes:* None whatsoever? *Mr. Sanchez:* None. *Nestor Sanchez before the House Foreign Affairs Committee* *August 3, 1983* The Aguacate airfield is a Honduran facility. We have no plans for its future use,	"A member of the Joint Task Force Command told us that on one occasion DOD personnel/aircraft [in Honduras] were used to transport ammunition for the CIA. In addition, U.S. Southern Command . . . officials informed us that the austere base, 8,000 foot landing strip, and the water system, constructed by the 46th Combat Engineers at Aquacate will be left behind for use by CIA personnel." *"GAO Responses To [Congressional] Questions In November 14, 1983, Letter," Report by the General Accounting Office* "Congressional sources with access to intelligence information said that U.S. aircraft had been used on ten to fifteen occasions in the past six months to ferry medical supplies, food and

nor do we plan any additional improvements to it." *Nestor Sanchez, before the House Subcommittee on Military Construction of the House Appropriations Committee March 7, 1984* **NOTE:** *DOD and the CIA claim that transfer of services is permissable, whereby one agency reimburses the other for those services once the costs are calculated. According to DOD and the CIA, classified agreements for proper reimbursement exist, however, the GAO was unable to obtain a copy of these agreements from either agency. Therefore, as of present date, it is impossible to verify if transfer of services, as in the case of Honduras, was appropriate, and if proper reimbursement took place.*	some military equipment to the anti-Sandinista forces . . . some of the flights carrying assistance apparently were coordinated with the CIA, since some of the aircraft landed at Aguacate, a contra base in Honduras built by the U.S. military for the CIA. . . . The sources said some of the supply flights involved aircrafts that were participating in joint U.S. Honduran war games. . . ." *Miami Herald September 7, 1984*

III. INFORMING CONGRESS ON MILITARY CONSTRUCTION

ISSUE: The Military Construction Appropriation Act of 1984 stipulates that for acquisition, construction, installation, and equipment of temporary or permanent public works, military installation facilities, none of the funds made available for airfield improvements in Honduras may be obligated until the Committees on Appropriations have been notified as to the complete United States construction plan for the region. Was the Congress properly informed and notified about the military construction which took place in Honduras during Big Pine II and was the Administration explanation for not notifying the Congress reasonable?

ADMINISTRATION POSITION	COUNTEREVIDENCE
Mr. Sanchez: Sir, we appreciate the fact that it has taken the length of time that it has to put this plan together, and we hope that when we do have the plan for you that it will provide you with the information that you are looking for, because the one thing we also want to do is cooperate with you. You have been cooperative with us . . . on the projects that	"The recent U.S. military exercise has created a substantial semipermanent military capability in Honduras. Congress has not been informed of this construction." *Unpublished report by the House Appropriations Subcommittee on Military Construction February, 1984* "Last year Congress passed, and the President signed into law a military construction bill which prohibited the construction of facilities at La Cieba,

ADMINISTRATION POSITION	COUNTEREVIDENCE
we have had, the construction that we have had in Central America, and we also want to reciprocate. We do want to get that to you ... I want to assure you that there is no underlying reason, other than the fact that we want to get the information together, it is being worked on ... and we are putting that report together for you and hope to have it for you as soon as possible. *Nestor Sanchez, before the House Subcommittee on Military Construction of the Appropriations Committee March 7, 1984*	Honduras, until the [Defense] department submitted a detailed construction plan for the Caribbean Basin region. Immediately following this action, the department, during the Big Pine II exercise, went ahead and constructed "training" facilities at six separate sites. This was done despite the Congressional action on Honduras." *U.S. Representative Bill Hefner, before the Subcommittee on Military Construction of the House Appropriations Committee March 7, 1984*

IV. THE NATURE AND PURPOSE OF MILITARY EXERCISES

ISSUE: The Reagan Administration asserts that military ground exercises in Honduras, in particular Big Pine II, and naval maneuvers, specifically UNITAS (June-November 1983) are routine exercises which are part of an ongoing training schedule which has been in process for years. Are these military maneuvers routine and part of a regular schedule, or were they designed to serve purposes other than the mere training of troops?

ADMINISTRATION POSITION	COUNTEREVIDENCE
"The simple fact is maneuvers are a very standard part of the Defense Department's activities. Exercises of all kinds are conducted all over the world on a regular basis. . . . These are exercises and they involve things that the military has done many times before on varying scales and varying years." *Caspar Weinberger, Secretary of Defense, to the Senate Armed Services Committee July 28, 1983*	"JCS and DOD officials told us that, except for NATO exercises, the United States does not generally leave facilities, materials, or equipment behind after training exercises overseas. . . . It appears that, . . . the leaving behind of facilities, materials, and equipment during AHUAS TARA II [Big Pine II] is a significant departure from past practices." *"GAO Responses To [Congressional] Questions In November, 1983, Letter," Report by the General Accounting Office*

ADMINISTRATION POSITION	COUNTEREVIDENCE

"[the exercises were] meant to be more than routine movements. . . . The decision to institute naval and ground exercises and have them occur at the same time and say they are routine begs the imagination."
Unnamed Senior Reagan Administration Official quoted in The Miami Herald August 14, 1983

". . . These are maneuvers of the kind we've been holding regularly and for years."
President Reagan, quoted in The Miami Herald August 14, 1983

". . . The stated purpose of these military exercises in Honduras has been the training of U.S. Forces . . . while in Honduras I was told by a high ranking U.S. official that another reason for the exercises has been and remains to bring pressure against the Sandinista government. . . ."
Senator Jim Sasser, statement issued February 8, 1984 following a trip to Honduras.

Reagan

"The purpose [of the military exercises] is training. It is an ongoing process."
Langhorne Motley, before the House Committee on Foreign Affairs August 3, 1983

"On July 8, a week before the Ranger was sent to Central America, Reagan met with his National Security Council to approve a range of military moves. The aim was to increase pressure on Nicaragua's pro-Marxist government to halt all support for leftist rebels in El Salvador. . . ."
The Miami Herald August 14, 1983

An NSC directive of early 1984 called on the CIA and DOD to continue naval exercises in Central America to "maintain steady pressure on the Nicaraguans" in order to "demonstrate a large commitment and resolve."
The Miami Herald February 1, 1984

Motley

GUATEMALA

Three human rights laws frame the pattern of U.S. relations with Guatemala: the Export Administration Act of 1979, the International Financial Institutions Act of 1977, and the Foreign Assistance Act of 1961. Since 1981, the Administration has circumvented the laws, or has attempted to seduce the Congress into overlooking the laws with misleading reports about the human rights situation in Guatemala.

I. MILITARY SALES

Section 376.14 of the *Export Administration Regulations* requires a company to obtain a license for the sale of military equipment. Military sales are prohibited to countries that are gross and consistent violators of human rights under the Export Administration Act. The removal of a military vehicle from the list of items that require a license simultaneously removes the equipment from under the ban on sales to human rights violators. On June 3, 1981 the Administration removed "vehicles specially designed for military purposes" from a Commerce Department list subject to Section 376.14 and placed them in a new category. This transfer enabled the U.S. to sell $3.2 million worth of military trucks and jeeps to the Guatemalan government of General Lucas Garcia.

II. MULTILATERAL BANK LOANS

Section 701(f) of the *International Financial Institutions Act* stipulates that the U.S. must oppose multilateral development bank loans to governments which are gross violators of human rights unless those loans serve basic human needs. Since 1981, the Reagan Administration has voted for twelve loans to Guatemala in the Inter-American Development Bank and World Bank, ten of which do not qualify as basic human needs loans. In an August 5, 1982 hearing to determine whether or not the U.S. would be in violation of Section 701(f) by voting in favor of an IDB rural telecommunications loan to Guatemala, Deputy Assistant Secretary of State Stephen Bosworth argued that the human rights situation had "substantially improved" to merit the loan. Bosworth praised Rios Montt's human rights record, but skirted reports of the Army's responsibility for widespread massacres in the Guatemalan countryside.

III. FOREIGN ASSISTANCE

Section 502(b) of the *Foreign Assistance Act* stipulates that human rights violators not be provided with security assistance or military exports unless the Administration certifies that compelling U.S. national interests warrant such aid. This would require that no funds be spent for training in a country where there is a pattern of gross and consistent violations of human rights. Because of 502(b) the Reagan Administration has been unable to increase the level of military aid and security assistance as outlined in its policy approach to Guatemala. In October 1984, however, the Administration managed to slip by Congress the sum of $300,000—a sum unmatched since 1977—for International Militiary Education Training (IMET).

I. MILITARY SALES

ISSUE: On June 10, 1981 the Administration approved a $3.1 million license for the sale of 150 military vehicles to the Government of Guatemala, including 100 half-ton jeeps and fifty two-and-a-half ton "cargo trucks." This sale was made despite congressional intent that military equipment not be sold to those governments considered to be "gross violators of human rights," as stated in Section 376.14 of the Export Administration Act. Did the Administration circumvent the Export Administration Act by transferring the jeeps and trucks from a list subject to human rights stipulations to a new list which was not?

ADMINISTRATION POSITION	COUNTEREVIDENCE

"In our opinion, the removal of these items [trucks and jeeps] from the crime control list and placement instead under regional stability controls is not inconsistent with congressional intent and does not undermine the provisions of the Foreign Assistance Act or the Export Administration Act."

Stephen W. Bosworth, Principal Deputy Assistant Secretary of State for Inter-American Affairs, before the Subcommittees on Human Rights and International Organizations and on Inter-American Affairs of the House Committee on Foreign Affairs July 30, 1981

"Now, when we reviewed a series of regulations under mandates from the Congress to reduce the restrictions on exports from the United States in order to improve our balance of payments, we found that these sorts of vehicles were on that list and were in demand in a number of areas. We made the decision quite independent of anything to

". . . no matter what the technical explanation was for releasing these trucks and jeeps to Guatemala—and the explanation is technically correct that they were taken off the police control list and that they were not subject to other restraints under the Export Administration Act, although they might have been but were not—but no matter what the explanation was, the perception is going to be that there again is another government which is engaged in, or at least permitting, a tremendous amount of violence in its country and that rather than tightening up on exports of items which certainly can be used in antiguerrilla operations we are expanding them."

Representative Jonathan Bingham, Chairman, Subcommittee on International Economic Policy and Trade, before the Subcommittee on Human Rights and International Organizations of the House Committee on Foreign Affairs July 30, 1981

"The refugees reported that the Guatemalan soldiers arrived in helicopters, trucks, and jeeps, and tortured and murdered innocent, unarmed civilians, including an 80 year-old-man and a 7 year-old girl. . . . By selling or giving the Lucas regime helicopter parts, training packages, or jeeps and trucks, we are literally aiding the indiscrimi-

ADMINISTRATION POSITION	COUNTEREVIDENCE
do with Guatemala to re-move them from that list." *John Bushnell, Deputy Assistant Secretary of State for Inter-American Affairs, before the Subcommittee on Human Rights and International Organizations of the House Committee on Foreign Affairs July 14, 1981* "I wish to assure the Com-mittee that human rights factors will be considered in reaching a decision on the ultimate disposition of these licenses and that these deci-sions will be in full compli-ance with the law." *Walter J. Stoessel, Jr., Under Secretary of State for Political Affairs, before the Subcommittee on Human Rights and International Organizations of the House Committee on Foreign Affairs July 14, 1981*	nate attacks on innocent peasant vil-lages and households." *Representative Don Bonker, Chairman of the Committee on Human Rights and International Organizations, before the Subcommittees on Human Rights and International Organizations and on Inter-American Affairs of the House Committee on Foreign Affairs July 30, 1981* "There is no evidence available that the Government (of Guatemala) has taken any effective steps to halt abuses or carry out any serious investigations of them. . . . In the past seven months not one person has been tried or con-victed for the killings of political fig-ures, priests, policemen, professors, la-bor leaders, students, campesinos. Kidnappings of members of these same groups average twenty-five a month." *State Department Incoming Telegram to the Secretary of State from the U.S. Embassy in Guatemala September 1981* ". . . I do not believe that there has been any marked improvement in the human rights situation in the last few months. Clearly we would have hoped there would have been." *Stephen W. Bosworth, before the Subcommittees on Human Rights and International Organizations and on Inter-American Affairs of the House Committee on Foreign Affairs July 30, 1981*

ISSUE: On August 8, 1983 General Mejia Victores overthrew the Rios Montt government. The Reagan Administration claims that under the new government the human rights situation has steadily improved, and that the continued improvement merits U.S. mil-itary and economic assistance. The Administration sold $3.2 mil-lion in helicopter parts to the Guatemalan government on January 7, 1984. Did the Administration violate Section 502(b) of the For-eign Assistance Act by selling these helicopter parts to Guatemala?

ADMINISTRATION POSITION	COUNTEREVIDENCE
Mr. Solarz: "And you[r] feel-ing is that the human rights situation in Guatemala has	". . . the conclusions readied in the [Organization of American States] Commission's report demonstrate that

improved sufficiently to justify this kind of assistance? [credits to purchase military space parts for 1985]?"
Mr. Motley: "The President's intent in backing the Bipartisan Commission report was to be faithful to its recommendations. In those recommendations was the element of military assistance to Guatemala.
. . . I think they are making progress. They are establishing an election. They have taken some institutional—it is a slow process, but they are moving in the right direction."
Langhorne Motley, Assistant Secretary of State for Inter-American Affairs, before the Subcommittee on Western Hemisphere Affairs of the House Committee on Foreign Affairs February 21, 1984

there has been no significant improvement of the human rights situation in Guatemala . . . disappearances, killings, torture, and the absence of [an] autonomous judicial system capable of insuring fair trials, render the rights in the American Convention on Human Rights illusory and are an affront to the conscience of the Americas."
The Inter-American Commission on Human Rights of the Organization of American States, "Report on the Situation of Human Rights in Guatemala," a resolution presented at the Regular Session of the General Assembly November 14, 1983

"First, the Guatemalan army has used helicopters extensively to subdue opposition in rural communities throughout the country. Second, human rights abuses have been endemic in Guatemala. . . . Third, and perhaps most important, the law of the United States (Section 502B of the Foreign Assistance Act) prohibits military assistance or commercial sales of military or police equipment. . . . We would therefore urge that you reconsider this decision to sell helicopter parts to the Guatemalan government. By cancelling this sale, the U.S. government could convey its continuing displeasure with the human rights policies of the Guatemalan government. Failure to halt this transaction, on the other hand, would only encourage the Guatemalan government to believe it can persecute its citizens with impunity."
Letter to Langhorne Motley from Republican Senator David Durenburger, signed by sixteen other Republican and Democratic Senators February 9, 1984
(in response to Americas Watch and Amnesty International reports on Guatemala)

II. MULTILATERAL BANK LOANS

ISSUE: In its first term, the Reagan Administration voted in favor of over $250 million in Inter-American Development Bank (IDB) and World Bank loans to Guatemala which do not qualify as basic human needs loans, as defined in Section 701(f) of the International Financial Institutions Act. In the past four years, Congress held only two hearings—in December 1981 and August 1982—on only one such loan: an $18 million IDB rural telecommunications loan to the Guatemalan government. In the December hearing, the Administration did not challenge Congress' assumption that the Guatemalan government was a consistent violator of human rights. Instead, the Administration argued that the loan served basic human needs. Did the Administration deceive Congress as to the purpose of this loan?

ADMINISTRATION POSITION	COUNTEREVIDENCE
". . . I would like to summarize the main factors leading the working group to conclude that the rural telephone service project serves basic human needs: The project is directed toward poor, rural areas; the majority of the benefits from the project will accrue to the lowest income groups; service will be for public use and small productive units; it will increase access of the poor to basic services, such as health care; and the project is an integral part of an overall rural development effort." *Ernest B. Johnston, Deputy Assistant Secretary of State, Bureau of Economic and Business Affairs, before the Subcommittee on International Development Institutions and Finance of the House Committee on Banking, Finance and Urban Affairs December 8, 1981*	*Mr. Patterson:* "You really cannot believe telephone service is a basic human need." *Mr. Johnston:* "No, certainly not. I do not think anyone would make that claim." *Ernest Johnston, before the Subcommittee on International Development Institutions and Finance of the House Committee on Banking, Finance and Urban Affairs December 8, 1981* *Mr. Patterson:* "Amnesty International and other organizations also report that the Guatemalan military routinely taps much of the country's telephone communications and the information goes to the country's security forces. How can you assure us that the expanded telephone system in this loan would not be tapped militarily in the fashion by the Government in the same way?" *Mr. Johnston:* "I do not think anybody could assure you of that, Mr. Chairman." *Ernest Johnston, before the Subcommittee on International Development Institutions and Finance of the House Committee on Banking, Finance and Urban Affairs December 8, 1981* "[Clerk's Note: On December 9, 1981 [day after the hearing], the Government of Guatemala withdrew its application for the telephone project loan from consideration at the Inter-American Development Bank.]" *Included in the text of the Subcommittee on International Development Institutions and Finance of the House Committee on Banking, Finance and Urban Affairs December 8, 1981*

ISSUE: On August 5, 1982 the Guatemalan government renewed its request. At this time, General Rios Montt was in power as a result of a military coup. It was the Administration's view that the human rights situation in the country had substantially improved under Rios Montt, rendering the basic human needs stipulation of Section 701(f) irrelevant. Despite lengthy testimony against the Administration's position, the U.S. voted in favor of the loan. Did the Administration attempt to mislead Congress into believing that human rights had improved under the Rios Montt government in order to justify voting in favor of the IDB loan?

ADMINISTRATION POSITION	COUNTEREVIDENCE

"I cannot emphasize strongly enough the favorable contrast between the current human rights situation in Guatemala and the situation last December when your Subcommittee held a hearing on this project. . . . In view of this marked change, the Administration is confident that supporting this loan to the new Guatemalan government is fully consistent with the provisions of Section 701 of the International Financial Institutions Act."

Letter to Representative Patterson from Stephen Bosworth, Principal Deputy Assistant Secretary of State for Inter-American Affairs July 15, 1982

"Thus with regard to the specific legal formulation which governs the U.S. voice and vote in the multilateral development banks, it is our very strong conclusion, Mr. Chairman, that while human rights problems do remain in Guatemala, that Guatemala cannot be considered by any standard of measurement to be a country in which there is a consistent pattern of gross violations of human rights."

"Human rights in Guatemala are once again being eroded by a return to repressive measures characteristic of former regimes. This is the conclusion of a mission of inquiry sent to Guatemala on July 21-25, 1982 by the American Association for the Advancement of Science, the National Association of Social Workers, the American Public Health Association, the American Anthropological Association, the Public Health Association of New York City, and the Institute of Medicine (National Academy of Sciences). . . . By most independent accounts, and occasional comments by Guatemalan authorities, the Army is not only engaging in stepped-up warfare against the guerrillas, but is once again contributing to the large-scale killings of non-combatant Indians in many places."

Dr. Jonathan Fine, Medical Director of the North End Community Health Center, Boston, Massachusetts, before the Subcommittee on International Development Institutions and Finance of the House Committee on Banking, Finance and Urban Affairs August 5, 1982

"On July 16, 17, and 18 [1982], in connection with my present work relating to Central American refugees, I traveled to the border area of the state of Chiapas, Mexico, near Ciudad Cuahtemoc, to visit Guatemalans who have fled their country and are now refugees. There are approximately 10,000 refugees in that area . . .

ADMINISTRATION POSITION	COUNTEREVIDENCE
Melvyn Levitsky, Deputy Assistant Secretary of State for Human Rights and Humanitarian Affairs, before the Subcommittee on International Development Institutions and Finance of the House Committee on Banking, Finance and Urban Affairs August 5, 1982.	Based on what I heard from the refugees, I would like to emphasize two main points: One, it is the Guatemalan Army itself which is causing the people to flee Guatemala, through its campaign of violence and terror in the countryside. Two, for the people in the countryside there has been no improvement since the March 23, 1982, coup and the violence against them has probably increased." *Angela Berryman, American Friends Service Committee, before the Subcommittee on International Development Institutions and Finance for the House Committee on Banking, Finance and Urban Affairs August 5, 1982*

III. FOREIGN ASSISTANCE

ISSUE: On March 23, 1982 General Efrain Rios Montt overthrew General Lucas Garcia in a military coup. Rios Montt's administration maintained power by implementing a state of siege on July 1, 1982 that suspended numerous freedoms previously granted by the Guatemalan constitution. Was there a "substantial improvement" in human rights under the Rios Montt regime as the Administration claimed in justifying its request for renewed aid to Guatemala?

ADMINISTRATION POSITION	COUNTEREVIDENCE
"[I]t is our conclusion that in terms of the actual events relating to the human rights situation in Guatemala that there has been indeed a very substantial improvement." *Stephen Bosworth, before the Subcommittee on International Development Institutions and Finance of the House Committee on Banking, Finance and Urban Affairs August 5, 1982*	"In the aftermath of the coup, Amnesty International has continued to receive persistent reports on an intensification of large-scale massacres of indigenous populations in the countryside . . . 2,186 killings Amnesty estimates took place between the time of the coup and the last week of June." *Ann Blyberg, Chairman, Amnesty International USA, before the Subcommittee on International Development Institutions and Finance of the House Committee on Banking, Finance and Urban Affairs August 5, 1982* "We have no scorched-earth policy. We have a policy of scorched Communists." *General Rios Montt, New York Times December, 6 1982*

"Now we have watched and monitored the implementation of that state of siege very carefully. We have not yet seen any actions taken under the state of siege which would change our basic conclusion that: First, there has been a significant improvement in the situation in Guatemala, and second, that it is not a situation characterized by a consistent pattern of gross violations of human rights."

Stephen Bosworth, before the Subcommittee on International Development Institutions of the House Committee on Banking, Finance and Urban Affairs August 5, 1982

". . . A separate decree also issued on July 1 established courts of special jurisdiction. These courts are an integral part of the executive branch and not part of an independent judiciary. These courts can order arrest or preventive detention of any person suspected of having committed a crime against the stated or public order. There is no right of habeas corpus for individuals arrested; freedom on bail is forbidden and the trials are held secretly.

. . . the state of siege permits searches without warrants, and the Government has used the state of siege to cordon off sections of Guatemala City and to conduct house-to-house searches.

. . . the right to peaceful assembly has been suspended.

. . . the Constitution of 1965 and the 1982 statute which replaced it both guaranteed freedom of movement, but under the state of siege such freedoms have been suspended."

State Department Country Reports on Human Rights Practices for 1982

"When there is a battle, we shoot at everybody alike, even though they don't have uniforms. . . . Practically all of them are guerrillas . . . so the order is to attack everybody alike."

Soldier in Cunen, El Quiche, Washington Post July 19, 1982

ISSUE: In mid-October 1984, $300,000 in International Military Education Training (IMET) was approved for the first time to Guatemala since 1977. In addition, the U.S. granted $12.5 million in Economic Support Funds (ESF) to the Guatemalan government, with the stipulation that the funds be used for development assistance for the poor, especially the indigenous population of the Guatemalan highlands. Due to the fact that no restrictions were placed on the $225 million Congress approved for the entire Central American region, the Administration can allocate up to $40 million in aid to Guatemala for 1985. Has the situation regarding human rights violations changed enough to grant the military assistance allocated by the Administration?

ADMINISTRATION POSITION	COUNTEREVIDENCE
"Now, the Mejia government has somewhat, I would say, to my surprise, continued a large number of the [human rights] improvements that Rios Montt began, rather than slipping back into the Lucas Garcia type of behavior." *Elliot Abrams, Assistant Secretary of State for Human Rights and Humanitarian Affairs, before the House Committee on Foreign Affairs* *May 16, 1984*	"The General Assembly . . . *Reiterates its deep concern* at the continuing grave and widespread violations of human rights in Guatemala, particularly the violence against non-combatants, the disappearances and killings and the widespread repression, including the practice of torture, the displacement of rural and indigenous people, their confinement in development centers and forced participation in civilian patrols, organized and controlled by the armed forces . . ." *Resolution of the United Nations General Assembly, Thirty-ninth Session, Report of the Economic and Social Council, sponsored by Austria, Canada, Denmark, France, Greece, Spain, Sweden: Situation of human rights and fundamental freedoms in Guatemala* *85 in favor; 11 against; 47 abstentions; United States cast "no" vote* *December 14, 1984*

Abrams

"But, I think there comes a time when you have to say look, we're going to have no influence over the behavior of the Guatemalan government and Guatemalan military if, in the face of improvements, in the face of an election that they are about to hold, we continue	". . . the number of persons tortured, murdered and forcibly abducted remains at an intolerably high level. The degree of brutality, accompanying these actions is noteworthy. The Catholic Church, trade unions, and University students are the targets of severe repression; as are all other persons perceived as fostering or expressing intellectual, political or economic inde-

to say that nothing has changed in Guatemala. That's just closing our eyes to the facts."	pendence. Similarly, the Indians of the rural areas remain a suspect class and continue to be subjected to severe persecution."
Elliot Abrams, before the House Committee on Foreign Affairs May 16, 1984	*"Little Hope: Human Rights in Guatemala, January 1984 to January 1985," Americas Watch Report February 1985*

"We are encouraged by the developments in Guatemala . . . We are proposing balanced economic and security assistance for Guatemala to reinforce the very encouraging democratic trends . . . Aside from its value in enhancing the professional and technical skills of the Guatemalan Armed Forces, the proposed IMET training will have the benefit of-exposing the military to American political institutions and ideals."

Langhorne A. Motley, Assistant Secretary of State for Inter-American Affairs before the Subcommittee on Western Hemisphere Affairs of the House Foreign Affairs Committee March 5, 1985

"There was an increase in the number of kidnappings and disappearances for 1984 . . . The security forces often take into custody suspects for questioning about subversive activities, while officially denying that they have done so. They almost always also deny knowledge of the whereabouts of the disappeared persons in response to inquiries . . . Whatever the mix of causes, overall disappearances and kidnappings with possible political motivations in 1984 rose to an estimated 425 compared to 307 for 1983."

State Department Country Report for 1984

APPENDIX OF POSSIBLE
VIOLATIONS OF LAW

The following U.S. and international laws -- some cited earlier in this report -- appear to have been violated by the Reagan Administration's policies toward Nicaragua and Central American countries. This is by no means a comprehensive list. The laws compiled here represent those which:

    a) have been possibly violated by the direct conduct of U.S. policy inside Central America, and which simultaneously

    b) have been misrepresented, circumvented or ignored by Administration officials during testimony before Congress.

A. Apparent violations of law resulting from U. S. Government assistance to the Nicaraguan contras

The Boland Amendment

The Boland Amendment originally became law on December 21, 1982. Until December 8, 1983, the Amendment prohibited the CIA and the Pentagon from engaging in military activities "for the purpose of overthrowing the government of Nicaragua..." In fiscal year 1984, the Congress prohibited funds in excess of $24 million from being spent by the CIA, the Pentagon "or any other agency or entity of the United States involved in intelligence activities" to be used to support "directly or indirectly, military or paramilitary operations in Nicaragua by any nations, group, organization, movement, or individual." From October 3, 1984 until October 18, 1986, the law banned all "direct or indirect support" for military and paramilitary operations in Nicaragua (save for $27 million in "humanitarian aid" and limited "intelligence sharing" and advice by U.S. intelligence agencies with the contras).

International Security and Development Cooperation Act of 1985, Public Law 99-83, Section 772 (d):

No U.S. government funds "shall be used to provide assistance of any kind, either directly or indirectly, to any person or group engaging in an insurgency or other act of rebellion against the government of Nicaragua."

Intelligence Authorization Act for Fiscal Year 1986, Public Law 99-169, Sections 101 and 105:

The conference committee report (House Report 99-373) barred U.S. intelligence agencies from:
"Participation in the planning or execution of military or paramilitary operations in Nicaragua by the Nicaraguan Democratic Resistance, or to participation in logistics activities integral to such operations."

The Neutrality Act

Dating back to 1794, Section 960 of Title 18 of the U.S. Code states:
"Whoever, within the United States, knowing begins or sets on foot or provides or prepares a means for or furnishes money for, or takes part in, any military or naval expedition or enterprise to be carried on from thence against the territory or dominion of any foreign prince or state, or of any colony, district or people with whom the United States is at peace, shall be fined not more than three thousand dollars or imprisoned not more than three years or both."

The Arms Export Control Act

U.S. Code, Title 22, Section 2778, states:
"Every person (other than an officer or employee of the United States government acting in an official capacity) who engages in the business of manufacturing, exporting, or importing any defense articles or defense services" must register with the United States government and must obtain a license. The penalty for failing to do so is $100,000 or two years in jail or both.

Intelligence Oversight Act

Requires that Congress be currently informed of intelligence activities.
Reporting Full and Current Information:
"The Director of Central Intelligence...shall (1) Keep the Select Committee on Intelligence of the Senate and the Permanent Select Committee on Intelligence of the House of Representatives

fully and currently informed of all intelligence activities which are the responsibility of, are engaged in by, or are carried out from or on behalf of any department, agency or entity of the United States, including any significant anticipated intelligence activity..."

Executive Order 112333:
Prohibits involvement of U.S. government in assassinations. "No person employed by or acting in behalf of the United States government shall engage in or conspire to engage in assassination...No agency of the intelligence community shall participate in or request another person to undertake activities by this order."

The Anti-Deficiency Act

U.S. Code, Title 31, Sections 1341 and 1350.
This statute provides that an officer or employee of the U.S. may not expend funds for unauthorized purposes and provides criminal penalties for knowing and willful violations.

Misuse of Public Money, Property or Records.

U.S. Code, Title 18, Section 641.
This criminal staute provides penalties for the use of U.S. money or property without legal authority, specifically for anyone who "embezzles, steals, purloins, or knowingly converts to his use or the use of others, or without authority sells, conveys or disposes of any record, voucher, money or thing of value of the United States or of any department or agency thereof, or any property being made under contract for the United States or any department or agency thereof."

Charter of the United Nations: Commitment to Non-Aggression.

Prohibits U.N. members from using force against other nations, except in individual or collective self-defense.

Article 2(3): "All Members shall settle their international disputes by peaceful means in such a manner that international peace and security, and justice, are not endangered."

Article 2(4): "All Members shall refrain in their international relations from the threat or use of force against the territorial integrity or political independence of any state, or in any manner inconsistent with the purpose of the United Nations."

Charter of the Organization of American States: Commitment to Non-Aggression.

Prohibits OAS members from using military force as an instrument of foreign policy except in individual or collective self-defense.

Article 18: "No State or group of States has the right to intervene, directly or indirectly, for any reason whatever, in the internal or external affairs of any other State. The foregoing principle prohibits not only armed force but also any other form of interference or attempted interference..."

Article 20: "The territory of a State is inviolable; it may not be the object even temporarily, of military occupation or of other measures of force taken by another State, directly or indirectly, on any grounds whatever."

International Court of Justice

On June 27, 1986 the World Court, in the case concerning U.S. military and paramilitary activities in and against Nicaragua, decided the following by a twelve to three vote:

"<u>Decides</u> that the United States of America by training, arming, equipping, financing and supplying the contra forces or otherwise encouraging, supporting and aiding military and para-military activities in and against Nicaragua, has acted, against the Republic of Nicaragua, in breach of its obligation under customary international law not to intervene in the affairs of another State..."

"<u>Decides</u> that the United States of America is under a duty immediately to cease and refrain from all such acts [against Nicaragua] as may constitute breaches of the foregoing legal obligations."

The United States is obligated to comply with the World Court decision by Article 94 of the Charter of the United Nations, which states:

"Each member of the United Nations undertakes to comply with the decision of the International Court of Justice in any case to which it is a party."

B. Apparent violations of law resulting from misconduct by U.S. officials

Fraud and False Statements

U.S. Code, Title 18, Section 1001
This statute provides criminal penalties for whomever "knowingly and willfully falsifies, conceals or covers up by any trick, scheme or device a material fact, or makes any false, fictitious or fraudulent statements or presentations."

Obstruction of Justice

U.S. Code, Title 18, Section 1501
This criminal statute provides for criminal penalties for whomever attempts to "influence, intimidate, or impede" the due course of the administration of justice, including criminal investigations.

Conspiracy to Defraud the United States and Commit other Felonies

U.S. Code, Title 18, Section 371
This provides penalties for two or more people plotting to violate criminal laws, such as those included here.

Misprison of Felony

U.S. Code, Title 18, Section 4

This statute provides criminal penalties for anyone who fails to report a felony, specifically "whoever having knowledge of the actual commission of a felony cognizable by a court of the United States, conceals and does not as soon as possible make known" the violation to the proper authorities.

Federal Election Campaign Laws

U.S. Code II, Section 431

This statute restricts and regulates the use of any funds in federal political campaigns. Prohibits the use of either foreign or federal funds in campaigns, and the 'laundering' of any such funds through third parties, such as political action committees, or 'PAC's'.

Misuse of Appropriated Funds for Publicity and Propaganda

Section 501 of the Departments of Commerce, Justice and State, the Judiciary and Related Agencies Appropriations Act of 1985, Public Law 98-411

Covered 1985 funding for the Department of State's Office of Public Diplomacy for Latin America and the Caribbean. Section 501 reads:

"No part of any appropriation contained in this Act shall be used for publicity or propaganda purposes not authorized by the Congress."

C. Apparent violations of law resulting from U. S. Government policy toward El Salvador, Guatemala and Honduras

See charters of the United Nations and the Organization of American States cited above.

1949 Geneva Conventions

Articles on the protection of civilians obligates the U.S. to insure respect of the conventions by other governments which the U.S. exercises influence upon.

Common Article I: "The High Contracting Parties undertake to insure respect for the present Convention in all circumstances."

War Powers Resolution

Requires the President to submit to Congress within 48 hours after U.S. forces have been introduced into hostilities.

Section 4(a):
"In the absence of a declaration of war, in any case in which the United States armed forces are introduced (1)into hostilities or into a situation where imminent involvement in hostilities is clearly indicated by the circumstances; (2) into the territory, airspace or waters of a foreign nation, while equipped for combat...The President shall submit within 48 hours to the Speaker of the House of Representatives..."

The Foreign Assistance Act of 1961

Human rights conditions on security assistance:

Section 502B(a) (2):
"Except under circumstances specified in this section, no security assistance may be provided to any country the government of which engages in a consistent pattern of gross violations of internationally recognized human rights."
Violations are defined in this section as "torture or cruel, inhuman or degrading treatment or punishment, or prolonged detention without charges or trial, causing the disappearance of persons by the abduction and clandestine detention of those persons and other flagrant denial of the right of life, liberty, or the security of the person."

International Security and Development Cooperation Act of 1981

Certification of military aid to El Salvador:

Section 728(b):
   "In fiscal year 1982 and 1983, funds may be obligated
for...El Salvador...and members of the Armed Forces may be
assigned to El Salvador...only if the President makes a certification
in accordance with subsection (d).
   (d) The certification...is a determination that the
Government of El Salvador --
   (1) is making a concerted and significant effort to comply
with internationally recognized human rights;
   (2) is achieving substantial control over all elements of its
armed forces, so as to bring an end to...indiscriminate torture and
murder...
   (3) is making continued progress in...land reform..."

Military Construction Codification Act

Limits on construction with military exercise funds:

10 USC2802(b):
   "A military construction project includes all military
construction work, or any contribution authorized by this chapter,
necessary to produce a complete and usable improvement to an
existing facility."

10 USC2805(c):
   "Only funds authorized for minor construction projects may
be used to accomplish unspecified minor construction projects,
except that the Secretary concerned may spend from appropriations
available for operations and maintenance amounts necessary to carry
out unspecified military construction projects costing no more than
($200,000)."

Export Administration Act

Human rights stipulations on military sales:

   Applications to export crime control and detection equipment
will generally be granted "unless there is evidence that the government of the importing country may have violated internationally re-

cognized human rights and that the judicious use of export controls would be helpful in deterring the development of a consistent pattern of such violations or in distancing the United States from such violations."

International Financial Institutions Act

Human rights conditions on loans:

Section 701(f):
"The United States Executive Directors...are authorized and instructed to oppose any loan, any extension of financial assistance or any technical assistance to any country described in subsection (a) (1) or (2), unless such assistance is directed specifically to programs which serve the basic human needs of the citizens of such country."

[The subsection referred to "countries...whose governments engage in a pattern of gross violations of internationally recognized human rights, such as torture or cruel, inhumane or degrading treatment or punishment, prolonged detention without charges, or other flagrant denial of life, liberty and the security of person."]

ABOUT THE EDITORS

Daniel Siegel edited this book as a Research Associate on the Central America Project at the Institute for Policy Studies. He is currently Director of Public Education on the Contragate Project at the Christic Institute, a public-interest law firm and policy center based in Washington, DC. He co-authored *Outcast Among Allies: The International Costs of Reagan's War Against Nicaragua* (IPS, 1985), co-edited *The Cuba Reader* (Grove Press, 1988) and was a contributing author to *Low-Intensity Warfare* (Pantheon, 1988). His work has appeared in the Los Angeles Times, Newsday, Des Moines Register and *La Jornada* (Mexico City).

Joy Hackel edited this book as a Research Associate on the Central America Project at the Institute for Policy Studies. She is currently a reporter. She was a Project Coordinator for Policy Alternatives for the Caribbean and Central America and was a contributing author to *Low-Intensity Warfare* (Pantheon, 1988). Her work has appeared in the Washington Post, the Los Angeles Times, Newsday and the St. Louis Post-Dispatch.